Open to Interpretation

This is an Artswork Book, produced by the Bath Spa University Press, Newton Park, Bath BA2 9BN, United Kingdom, in March 2008.

Designed & Typeset by Joshua Roberts / Wayne Smith

Printed & Bound by Athenaeum Press, Gateshead

Preface

We are very pleased and proud to bring you this collection of writing from students at Bath Spa University in England and Columbia College Chicago in the United States. This anthology was entirely devised and edited by students who participated in the first international exchange between the two schools. As you will see, the writing of these students is lively, vivid, and compelling; and we know that you will enjoy these stories and poems immensely.

The Bath Spa/Columbia College Chicago connection began in 2004 at the National Association of Writers in Education conference in York, England, when Randy Albers offered a demonstration of the Story Workshop approach originated by John Schultz, former chair of the Fiction Writing Department at Columbia College Chicago, and used successfully with undergraduate and graduate students for four decades at the school. A participant in that workshop, Carrie Etter, a faculty member at Bath Spa, was impressed, and visits were subsequently exchanged, involving Randy, Tim Middleton (Head of the School of English and Creative Studies at Bath Spa) and the Bath Spa Creative Studies Department Head, Steve May. The idea of a short-term exchange involving students and staff was hatched during these visits, and implemented during the 2006-07 academic year.

Four students were chosen from each school, all third-year undergraduates from Bath Spa and one undergraduate and three graduate students from the Fiction Writing Department at Columbia. Over the course of the year, through multiple email exchanges, occasional conference calls, and face-to-face meetings during two-week back-to-back visits between England and America, these students decided the theme and guidelines of the anthology, solicited manuscripts, read all submissions from both schools, discussed final choices, and edited the book. During the visits, they also attended classes, readings, and various late-night haunts in Bath and Chicago. The result of their conscientious and creative work is in your hands. (For anyone interested in the details of this exchange, maybe how to set one up yourself, a more complete description of the collaboration and its value for faculty and students may be found in the article by Albers and May, "A Transatlantic Writing Collaboration: Columbia College and Bath Spa University," published in the Winter, 2007, issue of *Writing in Education*.)

The Columbia mission seeks to help students "learn to author the culture of their times," and as the writing in this book amply demonstrates, students from the different cultures at both schools share this goal. Among its many functions, story helps define identity and constitutes a powerful mode of understanding that enables a bridging of cultural, racial, ethnic, socioeconomic and other differences. Today, writers need to see themselves as part of a global culture, not in the sense of a unitary or monolithic notion of that term, but rather as the meeting-ground of many cultures where understanding prevails, where all voices, even those not generally privileged in literary circles, can be legitimized and heard, and where conflicts can begin to be resolved. The work in this anthology stands, then, as a hope for a better world; and in the hands of these editors and contributors, the future of creative writing as a source for this meeting-ground of story is indeed bright.

International exchange programs carry enormous benefits for faculty and students alike, and this particular collaboration resulted in lessons and friendships that will last a lifetime. It has laid a solid foundation for other ventures planned for the coming years. As you read the work in this volume, we hope that you get some sense of the way in which the wings of imagination can carry all of us into other lands, enable us to hear the voices of other cultures, and set us on a course to establishing a better world.

Randy Albers
Chair, Fiction Writing Department
School of Fine and Performing Arts
Columbia College Chicago

Steve May
Head of Department
Creative Studies
Bath Spa University

Acknowledgements

The Bath Spa editors, Fliss, Debs, Liz and Lyndsey, would like to thank all the contributors to this anthology; both those that made it in to the final book and those that didn't. We enjoyed reading all the work we received; one book isn't enough to display all the writing talent at two fantastic institutions. We would also like to thank our friends in Chicago, who showed us such a great time while we were there. The hospitality and friendship we were offered will never be forgotten. And most of all we thank Steve May and Randy Albers, who gave us an opportunity of a lifetime in this project.

Administrative support on both sides of the Atlantic was crucial to the success of this venture. At Bath Spa University, special credit goes to Tim Middleton, David Coulby Director of International Programs and the whole faculty of the English and Creative Writing program. Support, both moral and financial, from Artswork, BSU's Centre of Excellence for Teaching and Learning, was crucial to the success of the project, and personified by the contribution of Dr Mimi Thebo, the senior teaching fellow. At Columbia College Chicago, particular thanks go to Provost/Senior Vice President Steve Kapelke for his visionary leadership in promoting international education, as well as to President Warrick L. Carter and Vice President for Academic Affairs Louise Love. Thanks, too, to former Dean of the School of Fine and Performing Arts Leonard Lehrer, present Dean Eliza Nichols, Executive Director of Academic Initiatives and International Programs Gillian Moore, Director of International Programs Chris Greiner, and the faculty of the Fiction Writing Department who welcomed and supported the Bath Spa contingent during their visit to Columbia. For production help essential to the completion of this book, as well as for other logistical and technical support, our gratitude goes to Matt Robertson, Sandra Heward and Karen Cooper at Bath Spa, and to Assistant to the Chair Deborah Roberts, Administrative Assistant Linda Naslund, and Secretary Nicole Chakalis in the Fiction Writing Department at Columbia College Chicago.

Editors

Katie Corboy
Felicity Crentsil
Debra Frogley
Liz Henley
Geoff Hyatt
Lyndsey Melling
Michelle Morrison
Jessica Young

It was Angela who first named Stuart's penis.

"He looks like a Horace," she said, tickling Horace playfully.

Stuart made Horace twitch. His pink tip bobbed up and down good-naturedly.

"He's nodding," he said. "He likes you."

Angela laughed. "Horace has good taste for a penis. Most of them are rather indiscriminate."

Stuart just had to kiss her. "Not Horace," he murmured into her coconut-scented hair. "Horace is a one woman penis."

"Well, I love you and Horace equally." Angela giggled, giving Horace a squeeze. "I hope you won't mind sharing me between you."

Stuart kissed her again. She really was the most unbelievably wonderful girl. He and Horace were incredibly lucky.

Later, he made her a cup of tea and brought it to her in bed. She took it from him with that little-girl look that ripped his heart into even smaller shreds.

"I'm sorry," he said, for the hundredth time. "This never happens. I don't know why. I am sorry, angel."

Angela smiled her most understanding smile. She was getting a lot of use out of it this evening.

"I do understand, darling. You don't have to go on. It happens to all men, or so I hear."

"Not to me." Stuart was afraid he might cry. "And not with you. Not with the angel."

Horace drooped, small and unrepentant, between them.

Three weeks later, and Stuart was at the bottom of a deep emotional well. There was no way out. The walls of the well were slick with Angela's excuses and slippery platitudes.

This wasn't about him. She had to concentrate on her career. There wasn't anyone else, how could he be so absurd?

She offered to return the earrings he had bought her. She gave him back his blue jumper.

Of course, she would always treasure the time they had shared. This was not, absolutely not, about Horace's refusal to function. All those recent nights, all those attempts to wake Horace from his coma, with hands, with tongue, with awkward dirty talk, all of those increasingly desperate times, were nothing at all to do with Angela's decision. It was her career. That was all.

Stuart slumped at his desk. From across the room, the door of vice-president Jake's office stood ajar. And from within drifted the voice of an angel. She was doing her most career-enhancing laugh.

Stuart could feel Horace, curled up and warm like a smug housecat between his legs.

It felt good to play squash with Jake that evening. He felt almost normal again. The squash courts were such a very male place for Stuart that Angela's absence was actually fitting for once. An acceptable absence, rather than a gaping, rotting hole.

He stripped off enthusiastically and headed into the communal showers. Jake was already there, soaping himself vigorously.

"Good game, Stu!" he called, boyishly. "You'll get me next time!"

"No, the better player won!" Stuart called back.

The hot water felt good against his skin. Revitalising. Maybe if he got back into shape Angela would want him again. Maybe he really should swallow his pride and see a doctor about Horace, like she asked him.

He looked at Jake, lathering up his copious chest hair. Now, there was a man in good shape. Stuart could never look like that, no matter how hard he worked out. Jake just had the better frame. Broad shoulders, rippling back muscles, firm, tanned buttocks. Stuart's eyes moved appraisingly up over Jake's body, until he arrived at the staring, unfriendly eyes. Jake flicked one contemptuous glance down towards Stuart's genitals and strode off. He left his soap. He left the shower running.

Stuart glanced down. Horace was awake. Awake and straining at the leash. He had been caught openly staring at his naked boss, with a fully engorged Horace.

Stuart arrived home exhausted and dumped his damp gym clothes in the utility room. He took a second shower to remove the smog and grime that coated his skin. Six miles home along the dual carriageway, in the drizzle.

He scrubbed his skin pink but the horror still clung to him. Jake's face, and Horace, and the shock of coming out to find Jake's car gone. Then the long walk home, knowing all the time that he would still have to face Jake at the office on Monday. He was coated with it. He didn't soap Horace. He didn't touch him at all.

After the shower Stuart felt a little better. At least Horace was still functional, even if he had chosen the worst possible time to wake up. He could never explain it to Jake, but then his boss was the kind of person to ignore uncomfortable things and pretend they never happened. If Jake wanted to cancel their Tuesday squash games, then so be it. He had been a bit smug since he got his promotion anyway.

There was one ray of hope. Maybe, if he could get her to listen, Angela might re-consider if she found out Horace was working again.

Stuart made himself a cup of tea and a ham sandwich. Halfway through spreading the mustard he realised he hadn't thought about Angela all the way home. All through that horrible walk and all the time in the shower, he had been so humiliated by Horace's thoughtless appearance that he had completely forgotten to be depressed. This thought afforded him a brief flash of happiness. Maybe he was getting over her. A millisecond later, he knew he was a fool. He would never be over her. Ever. She was an angel.

Stuart took his cup of lonely tea and his sad sandwich through to the living room and slumped into the chair. He thought of that first, unforgettable night on the sofa, when she had finally let him undress her. It had easily been worth the six months of excruciating head-games. He flicked on the TV. It would help him to forget.

He channel surfed, eating his sandwich without tasting it properly. At last he settled on the tennis. There was something relaxing about the back and forth, like a swinging pendulum in a hypnotist's fingers.

Sipping his tea, Stuart stared sulkily at Andy Roddick. That was the type of man Angela should be with. Andy Roddick would never have trouble in bed. He would sweep Angela off her feet and ravish her with the same macho confidence with which he handled his tennis racket. He looked a lot like Jake, actually. Stuart looked around for the remote control to blip him off. As he looked down, he realised that for the second time that day, Horace had reared his head and was fighting to get out of his confinement.

Stuart wept unconsciously as he ejaculated. He had been unable to masturbate to his old friends, the dog-eared pornographic magazines he had always returned to so faithfully. He had been unable to raise a smile from Horace for any of the new female porn he found spread-eagled on the Internet. Thoughts of Angela had done nothing, and she was the sexiest woman he had ever seen in real life. He shot his guilty, shameful load with images of Andy Roddick behind his eyes. Andy Roddick's tanned legs.

Jake's firm buttocks. Stuart wept, and Horace spat up.

By Monday, Stuart had made a decision. He would win Angela back. He wouldn't be daunted. He would work on the Horace problem, and in the meantime he would be the manliest man Angela had ever seen. His plan was a little vague, but the main thing was poise. Poise and attitude.

He didn't see Angela at all during the morning, but he kept up his poise and attitude so as to be ready for whenever she did make an appearance. He didn't want to be caught unawares.

He was waiting all day.

He ran into Jake in the lift, on his way out of the building. His poise and attitude faltered slightly. Jake smiled at him pityingly.

"Stu," he said. "Good to see you."

"Sorry about yesterday," Stuart began.

"Don't mention it." Jake said. He didn't apologise for leaving Stuart to walk home alone.

They both stared straight ahead. Stuart was very aware of Jake next to him, in that confined space. The silence grew. The lift was unbearably slow.

"Look, Stu, I have been meaning to tell you something." Jake was the one to look embarrassed now.

"Okay."

"It's just, well, Angela and I. We've started seeing each other. It wasn't planned."

Stuart felt as though Jake had hit him in the stomach. "You – and Angela." He repeated, dazedly.

"I wanted you to find out from me," Jake was saying. "I hope it's not going to be too awkward."

Stuart was sweating, dizzy. "When?"

"Oh… about a month."

"A month?" Stuart couldn't believe it. He and Angela had broken up only three weeks ago.

"Since the training conference. I am sorry it happened this way, Stu. I hope we can still be friends."

The lift doors opened and four secretaries piled in, saving Stuart the agony of replying. He and Jake moved to one side. One floor down, and they were joined by three more people. Stuart found himself jammed, sweating, against Jake, the man who had stolen his angel. Stolen her!

The rage was starting to rise, now. All this time spent feeling pathetic when he should have been furious! The minute they got out of the lift, he would punch Jake right in the face. In front of everyone! Hopefully Jake would have the decency not to hit him back.

Stuart was so immersed in his rage that he didn't feel Horace growing full against Jake's side, but Jake certainly did. He whirled around, forcing the secretaries to jostle each other. They shrieked. Then they noticed the bulge of Horace, and shrieked even louder.

Stuart looked down. He couldn't believe it. He literally could not make the mental shift between his rage and Horace's latest betrayal. He was in shock. He looked up stupidly, just in time to meet Jake's fist with his nose.

That night, in his pathetic bed, curled into a ball of self-loathing, Stuart couldn't sleep for a long, grey time. It hurt him to breathe through his nose. It hurt his nose and his pride equally. He was a battered man.

When he finally dropped off, he dreamed that he and Horace were walking along Jake's street, side by side. In the dream Horace could walk by himself, although Stuart didn't know how. It didn't seem important. What was important was that they had a common goal.

"You can have Angela." Horace told him. "And I can have Jake. We just have to make them see."

Stuart nodded. Horace was right.

"Let me do the talking." Horace said. "I can explain it so that they'll understand."

"Thank you." Stuart was filled with gratitude. Horace was on his side after all.

They reached Jake's house. The front windows were lit. They could see right into Jake's designer living room. There, more beautiful than Stuart had ever seen her, was Angela. Her pale, smooth limbs were spread out gracefully on Stuart's sofa, which had inexplicably found its way into Jake's house. And there was Jake, his tanned, firm body bending over her. Stuart let out an involuntary moan, in a burst of pure white pain.

He awoke with a jerk. He was wet. He was lying on gravel. He was lying on the gravel of Jake's driveway and the pure white pain had become headlights, coming right for his face. Stuart put a hand up to his eyes. Horace poked jauntily up through Stuart's fly, rain running down his pinkness in little rivulets.

Angela, sitting next to Jake in the front seat of the BMW, screamed.

Jake managed to stop just in time.

"Stay in the car, honey." Jake said, climbing out into the rain. He walked over to Stuart and looked down at him contemptuously.

"Get up," he said. "What the hell is wrong with you?"

Stuart pulled himself to his knees. Horace was still peering up at Jake.

"Cover yourself!" Jake snapped. "For god's sake, Stuart. I think I'm going to have to call the police."

"No…" Stuart managed, "Jake, please, you don't understand."

"Do you?" Pure disgust.

Stuart tried to stand, cold, numb hands trying to tuck the swollen Horace back into his trousers. It was at this moment that Horace decided to lunge for Jake. Stuart's entire body jerked as he was pulled forward by the groin, thrusting grotesquely. Inside the car, Angela screamed again.

When he woke up next, he was lying in an ambulance. His head hurt. He tried to move but strong hands pushed him back.

"Stay still, sir." A voice said. "You've sustained an injury to the head."

They kept him in hospital overnight. They gave him some pretty heavy sedative painkillers and he and Horace walked through his cloudy mind, bickering about whose fault this was. Stuart was pretty sure it was Horace's, but Horace claimed that Stuart had the greater responsibility, being in charge of the rest of the body. Eventually, they agreed to disagree. They were both in love. It was just a shame that they had such different tastes.

Thankfully, there were no charges laid against him and Stuart forgave Jake the assault. He was suspended from work for a month, pending investigation.

He and Horace spent the time quietly. They avoided each other as much as possible. Stuart's head was still very sore.

At the official company evaluation Stuart sat opposite an array of people, all of them his seniors, suffering gently. He had decided to be very quiet and contrite. He wanted his job back, although hopefully in another department. Maybe they would even let him work from home.

It was probably going okay, although it was hard to be sure. They heard the progress reports from the company psychologist. They heard from the people at the sleep clinic, where Stuart had been treated for his sleep-walking. Then they heard from Jake and Angela.

Stuart couldn't help weeping as he heard Angela talk of their short relationship. He hung his head and wept onto his chest, as her angel's voice filled the room.

Horace, for his part, leapt to attention from the moment that Jake stood up. He reared up, jerking Stuart forward, and began drooling immediately. Some of the drool soaked through Stuart's linen trousers. Stuart was crying too hard to notice.

It caused a bit of an uproar.

Later, when he and Horace were settled into the observation ward, they had a serious talk. Stuart explained that he and Horace were in two different places right now. They wanted different things. It wasn't working out. In the end they agreed that they would part ways. It would be best for both of them. Of course they would always treasure the times they had shared.

You fly each week between Chicago and South Carolina to be with your mother. You're her only daughter, her only child, her only blood left. She's lost even more weight since the last time. Now the white hospital sheets seem to cover pockets of air over a hollow skeleton. Last New Year, she resolved to lose weight, but not like this. She's lost a lot of things over the years. She lost her cool when you pierced your nose, and she lost her senses when she tore the ring out of your nostril. When Dad died, she lost the house and moved into an apartment too small to sneeze in. When you broke up with your last boyfriend, she brushed down her old wedding dress, sighing that it was too small for you anyways, and she lost it deep in the recesses of her closet. She lost her uterus in the spring, and it was a victory of sorts when the surgeons cut it out—"I wasn't using it anyways," she had muttered bitterly—but now she's losing again. She's losing white blood cells. She's losing time.

You close the hospital door and take your place in the plastic chair next to her bed. Her hair has been shocked white and brittle, her skin thinned into cellophane. "How are you feeling?" you ask.

From behind her oxygen mask, she shakes her head, No. You don't understand what that means. "No, not good?" Or "No, don't ask?" But you worry that it means; "No, I don't want to do this anymore. It's too hard. Breathing should not be this hard; living should not be a fight. What do I have left to live for? The house is gone. Your father is dead. The garden isn't ours anymore. I won't live to meet grandkids, to read your novel, or to stand at your wedding. I won't even live to see tulips. Tulips would have been nice. Tell the nice nurse to stop wasting her time with sponge baths. No. Just bring me red tulips one more time. I've had enough. How am I feeling? Honey, my final answer is *No*."

But you wouldn't take that for an answer. You would shout at her, "You don't have the right to be selfish! Not now. You owe me this. You owe me more time. You owe me because teenage years don't count. College years don't count. This counts now and you owe me. You can't say that it's too hard to try anymore. You can't. All you have to do is try. Just TRY."

But these words do not come from your mouth. Instead, you nod your head while she shakes hers. You smooth back her hair, and you fiddle with the pillow. You read her pages from your novel-to-be. In the tales that you tell, your characters live fast and die slowly. They get laid, get married, get fucked, get divorced, get screwed. You weave great plots and paint grandiose schemes. Your sentences breathe rhythmically like the accordion pumps in the tubes besides her bed. You trace the words with your pen like the steady stream of fluids into her veins, and you mark red edits that mimic the checkmarks tracking her pulse. The beeps from the monitor punctuate your pauses.

There is a break in the page.

You snap your head up to see if she's still awake. Her crystal blue eyes blink above the mask. The bedsheet rises and falls. The accordion of the pneumatic lung squeezes its noiseless music. Your mother lives on.

How much longer? How many more miles will you log? How many more nights will you spend on your mother's couch, too afraid to sleep in her bed? She's coming back, you proclaim aloud. You write your novel slowly, for what will happen when you have no more editing to do by her bedside? When will life go back to normal? What is normal supposed to be?

You tell your mother, "I have to catch my flight now. I have to go." You put your hand on top of hers, and she wraps both of hers around yours. Her hands are mottled, wrinkled, and frighteningly thin. You rub your thumb over her cool skin. She nods Yes, blinking in Morse code at you. You don't know if she understands, so you repeat, "I have to go now." Yes, she nods. "I have to go, Mom." Yes, she nods. Yes. Yes.

E

My grandparents had three large dogs—a Labrador who was fat, an English Setter who was sad, and an Irish Wolfhound who was just too big. The house belonged more to them than to people. Everything was covered in hair, banisters and doors were scratched, there were stains on the carpets, and on the top floor where no one had been for some time—shit. On the floor, the sofa, even in the bathtub.

That top floor, it was something else. Designed as a flat, it was being used as a dump. Everything smelt of dog or damp, or damp dog. There were broken chairs and heaps of newspaper everywhere. The textured wallpaper had once been white, but was now yellow and peeling, the grooves filled with dirt. In the kitchen sink potted Peperomia drooped, slowly dying.

My grandparents weren't happy. They were so unhappy that when I found out that Grandma had died I could not be sad for her, only myself. I imagined her as bright lights shooting through the stars. "Oh the joy of being free!" my dead grandma called, spinning and diving with no earthly bonds.

After the funeral I spent some time with Granddad. He'd had a stroke a few months back and though he could still walk, he could only move comfortably with the use of an electric wheelchair. I hadn't kept in close contact with him over the years; there had been a fight at some point, my parents barely spoke to him. But he could not be left alone to sort out that huge house, so I arranged to stay and get most of the work done—and for moral support, my boyfriend, Matt, came too.

Matt had made a list of the items in every room, ready to ask my granddad what he wanted, what was to be sold and thrown away. I got started with Grandma's room. Someone had straightened it a little. The sheets had been washed, the ashtrays emptied, and it was kept shut to the dogs. There was even a vase of Nasturtium on the bedside table—a strange gesture, I thought, such a cheery little flower.

None of Grandma's clothes were to be kept. I had two boxes with me— one for the charity shop and one for the bin. Hats and coats are easy enough, but when it comes to throwing out the underwear of someone who you loved… I wondered if my grandma had been concerned about what knickers she wore, whether she had thought that one day she would die and someone would go through that drawer. I wondered if she was watching me now, offended.

The next day I got up early to make breakfast for Granddad. The kitchen cupboards overflowed with tins and jars, all out of date. Caramelised oranges, mushroom soup and haricot beans, it all went into a black bag.

I took toast and a cup of tea to my granddad.

"You've run out of jam," I said. "Is marmalade okay?"

"Oh yes," he replied. "I like anything, apart from ginger." He considered his toast for a moment. "Even ginger is okay if it's not very strong." And then, softly, "Your grandma used to have vodka in her tea. I didn't realise for a long time, but she drank quite a lot. In her Cornflakes too."

I wondered what he could mean by telling me this; we had all known that Grandma was an alcoholic. Her own husband, however unhappy they were, however much they shouted rather than spoke, could not have been the only person unaware.

"I've thrown out quite a lot of stuff," I told him. "And everything that I wasn't sure about, Matt's put on a list. He's gone to speak to some people at an auction house, but he'll go through it with you later, if that's okay?"

"Oh yes, yes. I've got nothing to do."

I kissed him then, on the cheek. Because he was wearing dirty pyjamas that weren't properly buttoned. Because his face needed a wash and his fingernails needed cutting. Because there was shit on the floor and no food in the cupboards and he'd been eating out-of-date jam. Because he had lost his wife, whom he may have loved, even though they weren't happy. Because of all this, and because he was, after all, my granddad, I kissed him.

Then I went to town and filled the car with bleach and sponges, disinfectant spray, mould remover, carpet-cleaner and three stair gates.

Starting with the downstairs kitchen, I stripped and scrubbed every room, installing stair gates and locking doors to prevent the dogs from creating havoc the minute I turned my back.

I started off positively. I was working to make my granddad's life easier, healthier. I sang as I swept.

But as the hours passed, I began to cry.

I cried as I de-scaled the shower and cried as I bleached the toilet. At first it was for the effort and the fumes, but then the tears were for my grandma, who had lived in a dirty house and drank too much. Then they were for my granddad, all alone, even if he was happier that way. They were for my mother and uncles and aunts, who didn't speak to each other anymore. And then for my cousins, who I used to play with, but were strangers now—who I had chatted to at the funeral and who I wouldn't hear from again until the obligatory Christmas card. And then I even cried for those stupid dogs because it wasn't their fault that they were fat and sad and far too big. And as I cried I found myself making my way up the final flight of stairs.

It had been seven hours of solid cleaning by this point and yes, the house was cleaner, but it certainly wasn't clean yet. There were carpets to be taken up and tiles to be replaced, broken banisters and damp ceilings… Despite all this, I had been doing well… But suddenly, standing in that top flat, which was the worst of all, which really was something else, I stopped crying and began to scream.

A sheet of yellow wallpaper hung off the wall in front of me and I grabbed it, tugged it down, screaming as I did.

"Fucking house!" I screamed.

Sheet after sheet I ripped off the walls. Some came off whole; other bits in tiny shreds. I ripped at them with my fingers, getting my nails under the paper and tearing it down until my hands began to bleed.

"Stupid fucking house!"

Slowly all the junk was being covered in white paper and I liked that. I liked not having to look at all those beautiful broken things.

And then, before I knew it, I came to the final shred. And I stopped. I looked at that wallpaper, just hanging there, all limp and solitary. I thought that once someone had chosen that wallpaper, had spent a day putting it up. Someone else would have made tea, congratulated them on a job well done. Putting up wallpaper is so full of hope, I thought. And I sank to the floor.

Matt walked in on me, sitting there, crying on top of a mound of wallpaper. He didn't look shocked, he didn't ask questions – he just took my hand, lifted me to my feet, held me close and let me cry.

When I had finished he kissed the top of my head and kissed my eyelashes and we went downstairs.

That afternoon, smelling of sweat and disinfectant with paper in my hair and blood under my fingernails, we made love. Bodies entwined, fingers locked tight. A strange gold light formed around us, which I couldn't see, but I knew it was there. Matt's cheek rested against mine and as we moved slowly, so slowly, he whispered in my ear, "I love you. I love you."

Afterwards I curled up naked against him, rested my head on his shoulder.

"What are we going to do?" I asked.

"We're going to hire a skip and clean out this house. We'll take up the carpets and re-paint the walls and make everything okay."

"What then?"

"We'll go home."

"And what then?"

"We'll love each other. That's all anyone can do."

N

Peacefully he lies
on pebbles brown, and red, and grey,
in the cove on the coast,
where nobody goes;
rocks in clenched hands
and sand in his toes.

Peregrines circle him
eagerly, with hovering wing,
by the cliff, on the coast,
that nobody knows;
they stare with red eyes
at bounty bestowed.

Waves rush to him
angrily, grabbing at his skin,
on the small stony beach,
where no one has been;
they wish to wash clean,
things strange and obscene.

Silently he watches
with dead eyes, the birds and the waves,
in the cove, on the coast,
that only he knew;
waiting for saviours,
long overdue.

T

I bought the fairy soon after Heather finally dumped me. We'd been seeing each other for nearly two years, but I'd barely struggled past the "where is this relationship going?" question. She moved out, and without her craft tables and odd pieces of wood cluttering the front of the apartment, it felt empty; something needed to fill the void. I thought about pets.

Cats, dogs and birds were too ordinary. Fish were too easy. Turtles were depressing. It took a month of browsing pet shops before I found "Big Tom's Rare Books and Animals," nestled between a store specializing in Virgin Mary statues and a shut-down hardware store. The windows were so dirty, I might have thought it abandoned, except for the warm yellow light coming from inside.

Four tiers of shelves lined all the walls, stacked with glass aquariums, plastic habitats and cages. In the middle was a long table piled neck-high with old books; reading an open book on that table was Big Tom. He was round like a melon, and had the ponytail, glasses and too-casual clothes of a programmer.

"I'm Marshall," I said, shaking his greasy hand.

"Call me Big Tom," he said.

I told him I was looking for something unique, but which wouldn't require too much attention. He pointed to the nearest cage on the floor, which was also the largest.

"Wallaby. Like a kangaroo, but half the size. A lot of people like 'em."
I told him I didn't want anything that would take large craps. We moved on.

"These are cute—Vietnamese pot-bellied pigs. There's a lot of them around lately. You see, there was a kind of mini-fad for them, until people found out that they make a whole lot of noise, so now there's whole farms full of 'em. But you can litter-train them, they're smart..."

I took one look at the ugly, bristly thing and said, "No thanks." He showed me a light-colored fox with enormous ears.

"Fennec fox—easy to train—"

I cut him off: "Too much like a dog."

Big Tom patiently started on the second tier, above the big cages. Most of them had some sort of lizard, arachnid, or giant insect. Near the end, I saw a strange creature curled up in the corner – it had long insect wings, almost like a Japanese flying cockroach, but the body was tan and resembled a tiny human girl.

"That's a Brazilian fairy," Tom explained. "They can be difficult to keep."
He moved the plastic habitat from the shelf to a column of books on the

central table. The fairy was asleep on her side, in the fetal position, smaller than a mouse. She had messy black hair to her waist and a rich, tan skin tone. I pointed out the wings.

"I thought they had butterfly wings."

"Gaelic fairies have wings like butterflies, but they're endangered. Can't buy 'em anywhere. I had a whole litter of Brazilians in just a week ago, but I sold most of them on eBay. This one's the runt, so I'll sell it for $400."

So I bought it, without much consideration.

I never liked the idea of cages, so the first thing I did was get her out in the apartment. At two inches tall she fit easily in my palm. When I put her down somewhere, she would stay put. The only time she'd move was when I put the saucer of food near her. If I watched her, she'd only stare back at me, her mouth open and slack. Her head would track my finger or little objects moving back and forth, but she never showed any interest in pouncing or chasing anything.

She spent the first two weeks eating, shitting, sleeping, sitting and staring. One night I left an entire sandwich out on the coffee table, and the next morning it was gone, except for the crusts and the onions. Around the habitat, dotting the entire frosted-white glass table surface, were tiny fairy turds, which were surprisingly pungent.

Thus began my first foray into raising and housebreaking a live animal. I was working from home, typing up television transcripts, with all the time in the world to care for her, but she didn't seem to need any watching. I just had to wipe up her turds.

By week three, she started to fly. I'd been leaving her in the habitat in her nest of silk scraps (which is what most fairies preferred for bedding, according to the Internet), but one morning, before logging on to check my emails, bowl of oatmeal in hand, I checked her habitat, and it was empty. I poked the bedding scraps just to be sure, and my heart sank. That's when I started looking around frantically, first the table the habitat was on, then under it where the milk-crates of LP's might have caught her, then on the shelves; I checked under leaning books, just in case—but then I saw her, sleeping on top of the computer monitor. It made sense, being the warmest spot in the house (it was late fall, and my apartment was a drafty old rehab job). I left her there while I worked.

My job entails playing videos on the computer while I type, and I have two foot pedals, rigged up to rewind the video in two-second increments, when my typing can't keep up. The shows I transcribe are almost all political talk shows, all of the worst possible kind, featuring heavily made-up, glorified anchor people asking ill-informed questions, designed to serve the overt political agenda of the station that pays them. It's a horrible thing for an armchair leftist like me to be exposed to eight hours a day, but, at this point, their mumblings and inchoate phrases directly trigger the movement of my fingers, and I concentrate on the steady stream of letters and punctuation appearing on the screen.

It was about noon when the fairy woke up, probably when I turned the volume up on a particularly incoherent section of stammering TV people, and she promptly flew right past my face. That was my second surprise of the day. I swiveled my office chair, and saw her touch down in the middle of the floor. She took a few uncertain steps and then made a pathetic jump. Her wings flapped, sounding like the fluttering of paper stuck inside the cage of a fan, and she gained about a foot of altitude before descending back to the floor. She was nearly beneath the table of her habitat. She made one more attempt, then sat down abruptly.

I rushed over, and she looked at me with an abject expression. I held out my hand but she just stared, so I nudged her until she was a sad little pile in my hand, and delivered her to her nest. I also noticed that she weighed a little more, and seemed taller, maybe an inch, bringing her stature to a whopping four inches. My fairy was growing!

A month after buying the fairy, I named her, "Picky," since she preferred wheat bread to any other kind, and out of all the cold cuts, would only eat turkey breast, and never the onions. She also started a new behavior: singing. It wasn't anything special—tinny humming in random, atonal notes—but it was endearing, like a dog learning to beg for food.

This is also the time that I started speaking to Heather again, regularly. She'd call, reminding me that I needed to put my name on the electric bill or something, and I'd remind her that I'd done it already, at which point we ran out of things to say. After a week of these "clean-up" calls, we were ready to be friends again, and I met her out at bars a few times.

Heather still looked good to me. She kept her blond hair chin-length, purposefully messy, and managed to look fashionable despite her butt getting bigger. Thirty was looming in her future. She had those sleepy kind of eyelids which never failed to turn me on when I noticed them. It was what I called "permanent bedroom eyes syndrome," and I got a kick out of how many dudes would try to pick her up when we were out together.

"I'm not dating anyone yet," she reported to me, at a bar neither of us frequented—too many yuppies, too much emphasis on martini drinks—but there was privacy in anonymity. She had stopped listening to me, just waiting to ambush me with this news about her dating status. It was one of those moments that lasted too long, because I didn't know what to make of her statement; if I should care, or be jealous, or competitive...

I nodded and said, "I've been too busy to think about it."

"What's been keeping you so busy?"

I told her about my pet fairy.

"Aren't those an endangered species or something?"

"No, not the Brazilian ones."

Heather asked the usual, about what it ate, how much, if it was housebroken, etc. which you know already. Then she asked if she could see it sometime.

"You can come over if you want," I said.

"Are you ready for that?"

"Are you?"

Heather shrugged, and finished the rest of her beer. This was the way she acted in the waning part of our cohabitation: pretending not to care, but only later revealing that her nonchalance was some sort of test for me, as if to see how well I could read minds. I always insisted that any test based on intentional deception (i.e. her feigned indifference) was automatically invalid. She didn't agree, and that's why we split.

Heather dropped by unannounced a few days later, which I had said would be OK. I was at the computer, and hearing the lock turn, I knew I didn't have to get up. Picky, now six inches tall, was on my shoulder—her new perch of choice—watching the videos of talking heads playing on the computer screen. I didn't want to dislodge Picky, so I just called out, "Hey, Heather."

"You still have those cans of Minwax, right?" Heather's hobby was cabinet making, and having left many supplies behind, it seemed a valid question to me.

"Yeah, should be in the same place."

There was no need for me to move, so I kept working.

I heard Heather rustling around in the rear of the apartment, then come back, setting some cans down on the coffee table.

"Oh, is that your fairy?"

Heather hovered over my left shoulder, looking. I assumed that Picky was giving Heather the usual vacuous, open-mouthed stare. I stopped the video I was transcribing and looked to Heather, who was frowning.

"What's up?"

"It's…" Heather huffed and stood up straight. "It's *naked*."

"*She's* an animal. You don't make your dog wear a sweater, do you?"

"That's different. Titus is a *dog*." Heather leaned close again. "Hello? Do you talk?"

"Sometimes she sings," I told her.

"What, like radio hits?"

"Kinda like a bird. No words, just a bunch of I dunno, *notes.*"

Heather didn't say anything, which meant she was holding something back. The corner of her mouth curled up, accentuating the faint laugh lines she was so self-conscious about.

"OK, what?"

"It's really creepy," she said. "I mean, it looks just like a little girl. And it's just hanging out on your shoulder, like, totally naked."

"Like I said, she's an animal. They just look like little people."

"You should still get it some clothes. I mean, don't you think it's a little perverted to have a naked girl-looking-thing flying around your apartment?"

I honestly did not consider it until then, so I didn't answer Heather.

"Can I pick it—*her*, I mean—can I pick her up?"

"Yeah, but don't grab her. She doesn't like being handled." That I knew from Picky's bath sessions—I had to hold her down in the water with one hand, and scrub her with a soapy Q-tip. All the while Picky would protest in shrill tones, somewhere in the vocal range of a mouse.

Heather put her hand out, and Picky had at enough awareness to climb on Heather's open palm and stand there.

"Look, she's even got pubic hair."

I looked, and saw minuscule black hairs for the first time—easy to miss, but it seemed my fairy was hitting puberty.

"Yeah, I'll get her some clothes."

I decided that Picky could wear doll clothes, from the local corporate toy mega-outlet. From the pink-festooned, bright-eyed, and supposedly gender-role-positive section, I brought a pile of glossy pink-and-glitter colored boxes to the checkout, along with a gigantic, expensive box containing the three-room bungalow of the same brand, matching the figurines of large-breasted, small-waisted, perpetually smiling, and high-heeled dolls. I didn't get the Corvette, though. The girl working the checkout didn't even look at my face, saving me the unlikely explanation of saying, "For my niece". I bought the doctor model (rather than the nurse), the evening wear version (the dress looked easy to put on), the "Rosie The Riveter" commemorative doll, and after some deliberation, the flight attendant. The total made me wince, but I handed over my card, remembering Heather's disapproving scowl.

I hated those silly dog sweaters people put on their Scottish terriers (even worse, the miniature plaid golf cap). Seeing animals humiliated like that just pissed me off. I supposed fairies were different, because they don't have fur coats. I could be a fetishistic maniac, but I'm sorry, a nine-inch-tall girl with beetle wings just didn't turn me on.

Anyhow, Picky didn't like the clothes. I had to cut slits in the backs of the tops in order for her wings to fit, and I was forever finding the doll clothes on the floor. When I did manage to force her to wear them, they looked awfully uncomfortable – they were baggy and stiff, and to Picky they must have felt like sweaters woven from sailing hawsers.

But that wasn't the biggest problem. The problem was she outgrew the clothes in two weeks. She was twelve inches tall, and starting to get clever. By clever I mean annoying.

I'd gotten clothes from slightly larger dolls, so Picky was traipsing around in a balloonish pair of blue, star-spangled pajamas. While I worked, she would run—the apartment was getting too small for her to fly in— from the front room, my office, down the hall into the kitchen, and then run back again, sometimes adding short, buzzing flights. Every few laps, she'd crash into something, like the bookshelves that lined my office/ living room, knocking over piles of books, scattering papers, upsetting jars full of paper clips, spilling pens, dumping glasses of water or unfinished beer bottles, and generally being a nuisance. This, I understood, was the problem with all young animals, but I started not to think of her as an animal, rather as a small, retarded person.

She would make it onto the computer desk and jump on the keyboard, or start hitting buttons with her fists. I'd grab her by the middle and set her down on the floor, gently, but each time with less and less patience. At night I'd wake up from her wings tickling my face; she slept in a nest on the couch, but would clamber over things at night. I'd hear cupboards slam open, a box of cereal tumble down, and then for hours, tiny munching noises, while I kept readjusting my pillow.

Heather kept coming over. She'd make excuses, like her printer wasn't working, or she'd forgotten something and wanted to look for it. And after about five minutes of enacting the excuse, whatever it was, Heather would make herself comfortable by reading a magazine, making tea, using the bathroom—sometimes with the excuse that the hot water at her place had no pressure. Heather would eye Picky running around, but never interact with her. Mostly my back was turned to these visits, trying to keep up with work, but sometimes I'd catch Heather staring after Picky with a sour expression. It bothered me, until I figured out what it was.

"You're jealous," I said, without turning around. Heather was on the couch reading a novel.

"No I'm not." Her response was too quick to come, and I think she realized it. "How could I be jealous of that thing? We're not even dating."

"Are you dating anyone?" I asked.

"Not really."

"What's 'not really' mean?"

"I mean I'm not seeing anyone *seriously.*"

I knew she wasn't one to pick up random guys in bars for one-night stands, but I was feeling mean, so I said, "So you're just sleeping around, then?" There was a satisfying silence.

Then she said, "At least I'm not sleeping with a one-foot-tall, retarded animal."

My fingers froze on the keyboard. I felt blood in my temples.

"Next you're going to say something about the size of my dick, aren't you?"

"No. You think everything has to do with your penis."

This made me turn around and face her, which is what swivel-chairs seem to be made for.

"Why are you hanging out here?" I asked her.

"Fuck." Heather shut her book and stuffed it into her backpack. "You know, I thought we could be friends, at least, so I'm just trying to be friends with you. If that's not going to work..." Heather shrugged, and started putting on her jacket.

"Hold on, I was just asking why you always give Picky dirty looks." I looked over at Picky, who was using a spaghetti noodle like a whip, to punish a duck-shaped doggie chew toy. Her clothes were covered in spaghetti sauce.

"I don't care about your pet fairy. It's just a creepy-looking animal." Heather looked at me for a response. I just gave her a resigned look, like she was making a moot point.

"Hello!" said Picky, in her tiny, tinny voice.

Picky was talking, and I tried to talk to her. Unfortunately, since most of the voices she heard were from TV news and talk shows, she would say things like, "I see," "coming up," "police," "terror," "Iraq," "President Bush," "speaking of," "homeland," and "market." There was no context for her to learn from, since there were just talking heads on my computer screen, and I was always quiet, trying to keep my typing up. She didn't form sentences. She'd be on the top bookshelf, methodically pushing one book after another off the shelf, saying "Terror!" or "I see!" each time a book hit the ground.

I had to make a business trip to San Diego. Never mind that I worked from home, and was a self-employed sub-contractor. Sub-contracted to our clients, and had no real need to go out to San Diego, but corporate policy demanded it. Since she was still *technically* my best friend, Heather agreed to fairy-sit for me, for a week.

I have come to the following conclusions about what went on in my apartment while I was gone:

- Heather must have brought over three or four gallons of ice cream, but instead of eating it, decided to smear it across all surfaces of the kitchen.
- Heather must have brought one of her fashion designer friends along.
- Heather must have brought over a ton of movies that she likes, probably involving subtitles.
- Heather didn't just come over to make sure Picky was OK, she stayed over.
- She didn't stay there alone.
- Heather slept in my bed.
- She didn't sleep in my bed alone.
- Heather must have ordered about two hundred pounds of Chinese, Thai, Indian, Mexican and Pizza.
- Smoking pot makes fairies grow faster.

These conclusions were evidenced by:

- Picky was wearing a red tube top, black arm warmers, tight plaid pants, combat boots, lipstick, mascara, and one of the aforementioned plaid golf caps I hate to see on Scottish terriers.

- Picky, though still not making sense, was saying things such as, "promise me," "relationship," "forever," "Aye Madonna!" and "L'amour est pour toujours!"
- My pillowcases smelled like Heather's shampoo.
- My sheets smelled like cologne.
- There were ripped condom wrappers stuck between the mattress and the wall.
- There were two trash bags, spilling over with take-out boxes, pizza boxes, beer cases, and Styrofoam containers in the kitchen.
- The whole apartment smelled like bong water.
- Picky was now three feet tall.

My arrival home: slack-jawed, numbed by the three hour flight and subsequent train commute from O'Hare, I stumbled from one room to another, mentally tallying the damage, and came to stop in the living room. Picky was sitting on the couch, across from the blaring TV, painting her toenails—meaning that in the process of painting her *toes*, her toenails were also covered. Months later, I was still finding red toe-prints.

There was a note on the fridge: "Sorry, I didn't have time to clean up before you got back, I'll make it up to you. Heather."

I cleaned up.

From that point on, Picky seemed more like a weird small person than a child. She'd watch television, quietly, make herself a sandwich every once in a while, even read books. One morning I saw Picky open a window, fly out, and when the sun was setting, when I'd already decided she wasn't coming back, she buzzed back in.

Picky didn't talk to me, and I didn't try to talk to her, because she looked angry or supremely bored. We were like roommates that were stuck together, despite some smoldering grudge. When she was four feet tall, she got a job at a courier company, flying small packages around downtown. Of course, she was being paid under the table, but everyone thought a fairy delivering packages was cute, so nobody called the IRS.

We lived on different schedules. Picky was out while I worked during the day, and I went out to bars, usually with Heather, until midnight. I'd wake up, sometimes, when Picky came in around four in the morning, stumbling around and knocking things over—God knows where she was hanging out—and she'd pass out on the couch until noon, then buzz out the window. Some nights she didn't come home.

It was late in October, with the re-election of Bush looming—I predicted it, though I despised him—and I met Heather at the bar we frequented together. I wasn't boring her with election-talk, and she wasn't pretending to check out other guys to get me jealous.

"How's your place—I mean, your roommate?" I asked.

"I can't stand her anymore. I'm going to look at a studio this weekend."

"Cool, where?"

"In Pilsen."

Pilsen was the opposite end of town. It would be hard for us to see each other.

"We could always try again," I blurted. Eight beers will do that to me.

"What?"

"You could move back in."

"Yeah, I could." She looked away, playing with her bottle.

"Do you want to go back there—to my place?"

"What, now?"

"Yeah, why not?" I couldn't help but grin.

"No." Heather looked as if she'd just caught a chill. Nothing was going to happen between us again, not ever. There wasn't anything left for us to talk about. Not the terrible movies Hollywood produced, not mutual friends and their problems, not unfinished projects or ongoing hobbies, not popular books that we both hated, not TV shows that had turned out a bad episode—not a thing left to discuss. My universe shrank like a leaking balloon. Heather looked far away, across the table, reserving herself for someone else, some other life.

I finished my beer and left.

I got home and sat on the couch, drained and sobered from the chilly walk. I stared at the wall, feeling again like Heather dumped me again, though we never got back together. I didn't cry, just felt an ugly cloud descending on my shoulders, into my chest. It was like I'd lived weightlessly my whole life, and for the first time I felt gravity.

I must have sat there for a long time, because the next thing I noticed was the window slamming open and Picky tumbling through. She giggled and sprang up, tossing her long black hair back. She had a wild, drunken stagger and regarded me with half-open eyes and a sneer. She was taller than I remembered—five feet eight, I think—she wore a black sleeveless top with a big zipper down the front, black skirt with a gigantic studded belt, and tall boots with three-inch heels. Other than the gigantic insect wings, she looked like a young Brazilian woman just getting back from a night out. I stared, slack-jawed, not thinking but just seeing her.

"Marshall," she said. "Marshall..." She bent over, unzipped her boots and blundered out of them. She sat down on my lap, running one hand over my shoulder and the other in my hair. Our foreheads touched. "I like you," she said, and I heard the accent. "I like you," she kept saying, and we kissed.

Picky had been living the city life, hanging out with guys, probably at the Latino clubs I never went to. She used a lot of Spanish words, between sucking on my lip greedily, then moving on to my ear, rocking her pelvis into me, her arms caressing, pulling on my T-shirt, while I leaned into her, pulled the big zipper down the middle of her top, sucked on a large, dark nipple, pushing against the floor and the couch, so we could stand together, undressing each other—my jeans with attached keys hitting the floor, her skirt swishing off. I stopped for a moment to look at her, in her underwear (black, of course), with my hands on her perfect waist, the smoothest skin I've ever touched, and got a look at her face – sharp nose, sharp jaw, sharp eyebrows (plucked, I think), and the dark pools of her eyes, onyx with a violet glare – and she pitched forward to attack me with her tongue, everywhere and downward, lips grazing the hairs down my stomach, to the head of my cock. She got me fully hard with her tongue (the alcohol delayed my response a little), then slipped on a condom in two quick, downward strokes. Her expertise amazed me.

We had sex on the sofa, the coffee table, skidding across the floor, then against the wall, then over the arm of the sofa, and then a final bout, shouting and shoving together on the floor again. It took me a long time to climax, because of all the beer, but it was just enough, and the release was one of those I call a "Level Two," which means I felt it in my stomach and the back of my head. She had come a few times herself, each with a long "*nnnnnnngh!*" and after I withdrew, she kept talking to herself in Spanish, then got up, beat her wings once, and went to the bathroom.

I was sweating profusely and I wanted to take a shower, possibly with her, but the bathroom door was locked so I went into the bedroom and lay down. All I could think of was that it was better than any sex I had with Heather, and I dozed off.

The next morning I woke up—no hangover—put on some boxer-briefs and went to the kitchen. Picky was hunched over on a chair with a white bathrobe on, her shoulders shaking. On the floor in front of her were two long, translucent insect wings. I sat on a chair next to her, put my arm around her, and she cried for an hour.

Later that day, Picky packed her clothes and few belongings into luggage I gave her. She said the wings just fell off sometime in her sleep, and showed me two scars above her shoulder blades. I kept asking her to stay, but she kept shaking her head and her eyes never dried out. In the evening, she made a phone call, in Spanish. Sniffling, she said goodbye, thank you for being nice, et cetera, and left, using the front door.

She had left the wings in the kitchen, so I crumpled them, dry and crackling, and threw them in the garbage.

I tried to do some work, couldn't concentrate; made some coffee; listened to music, but nothing seemed appropriate; tried to read a book, failed; and was quickly descending into the deepest depression of my life when the phone rang. It was Heather.

"I really want to say sorry," she said.

"For...?"

"For rejecting you last night. I was just... I don't know. I get defensive sometimes, you know? It was just a surprise."

"It's okay," I said. My heart beat six times, and then I said, "I love you, you know?"

"Yeah. I love you, too."

"You want to come over to talk?"

"Yeah, we should talk."

"That'll be good."

"I'll be there soon."

I hung up and waited for her.

Emerson Leese   Morning Has Broken

I awake to the sound of shouting. Always shouting. Never once do I wake to the soothing sound of angels whispering sweet delicacies by my ear. No, just the same gruff Scotsman with his less-than-dulcet tones reverberating around what's left of my mind.

"It's nine o'clock gentlemen. Wakey, wakey!"

More shouting. Different voices, wordless sounds.

"Let me sleep for god's sake!" One voice prays, under his breath.

"Fuck off Doug!" Another retorts, yet quieter, more hushed, for fear of being heard.

"Have I missed breakfast yet?" A common question.

Different sounds, wordless voices. The same noises that I've heard every morning now for the past two years. I slowly open my eyes, eyelids pulling apart the sandman's gift to expose dilated pupils and raw emotions.

I consider pulling the duvet over my head and hiding from Doug as the child hides from the bogeyman. It seems more than a little unfair that the duvet can protect you only 'till a certain age; from then onwards you're on your own.

"Come on people, everybody out of bed! Don't let me have to tell the Captain that you lot have been playing me up. You know how much he likes putting people back on the streets!"

Doug. Always Doug. Allow me to introduce Doug. Doug's a corporal in the Salvation Army. He also works for the S.A. as a project worker in a homeless hostel in London's east end.

I live in the same hostel. As you can imagine, I use the word 'live' in its loosest form.

Doug also happens to be one of the most sadistic human beings that I've ever come across. He gleans great pleasure from belittling and intimidating the lost and lonely souls that make their way into his life.

Doug and I don't see eye to eye.

He considers that his approach to social work befits not only a Salvation Army officer, but also a good Christian soldier. I consider him to be one step below a prison warden on the great chain of being. But then again, I'm biased.

I hear Doug knocking on a door a few away from mine.

"Come on gentlemen, another beautiful day in the opera of the homeless."

I consider my options:

1. Feign an illness, thus allowing me to stay in bed while the hostel cleaners clean the other resident's rooms.

2. Get up. Have breakfast, slouch around the hostel all day.

3. Get out of the hostel and make something of my life.

Let's deal with number 1 first. For Doug, nothing short of throwing up a kidney would do to convince him that I was ill. I try a little cough to see if this is a possibility. No kidney is forthcoming. Number 2. Mmm… this would be a little more interesting if I hadn't been doing it daily for over two years. Talk about going nowhere. Which leads us directly to option 3:

Getting out of the hostel and making something of my life.

If only it were that easy. This is my life. Up at nine. Morning prayers followed by breakfast at ten and then finding ways to fill your time until dinner at five. Then it's evening telly and bed by eleven.

Spontaneity is a word that left my life long ago

I hear a knock at the room next to mine. He's getting closer: I'm running out of time. I try to think around the problem, to 'think outside of the box' as the counsellors who visit us are fond of saying. Yet all that I can hear is a phrase from the serenity prayer that is spoken at the daily Alcoholics Anonymous meetings that are held here: "God, grant us the serenity to accept the things we cannot change."

I cannot change the ebb and flow of my life. I've tried before. I've tried and failed. It's got to the stage where I don't consider *trying* to be an option. Let's bin option 3. It's easier all round.

A knock at my door.

Silence.

Another knock, and this time I hold my breath, praying for Doug to be on his way, to forget that I exist in his world. But God stopped answering my prayers long ago.

"Captain Richards?" Doug's voice, softly.

I sit up in bed, the inevitable unavoidable.

"Captain Richards? The residents are all ready for morning prayer."

"I heard you the first time Doug," I reply. "I'll be downstairs directly."

Wentworth Village reminded me of a bullseye. Fields surrounded the village and in the center there was the town square with a gazebo where a string quartet used to play during the warm weather when tourists still flocked to the village. Pick any of the dirt roads and it will take you to the gazebo.

A group of grade school kids clustered around a very pregnant young guide who walked with one hand pressed to the small of her back. "They must be off to the barn for the milking demonstration," I said to Mrs. Bloome as we both took a break from our chores to watch the group. Beyond them I saw Sarah Silver, who lived in the park with her family, skip by with long twin braids trailing from under her bonnet. Her ankle-length paisley dress and plain pinafore clashed horribly with the students being led by tour guide Beth. Those students paused to turn wide eyes upon every horse tied to a hitching post and every clapboard house that lined the street leading to the dairy farm around which Wentworth Village grew up.

Mrs. Bloome shook her head and sighed at Beth, who dropped out of high school not that long ago to marry her childhood sweetheart and to paint. Mrs. Bloome went back to hoisting a large roasting pan, heavy with a pale turkey, off the counter and into the waiting Glenwood Grand cook stove—a massive heap of cast iron that filled most of the kitchen— while muttering to herself.

She took a small towel from her apron strings and wiped it across her forehead. My bonnet prevented sweat from trickling down my forehead, but stains formed under my arms. The cook stove produced no heat, but the sun coming in through the glass west wall of the kitchen baked us.

Currently pressed against the glass wall were about fifteen preteen kids wearing bright orange t-shirts. One boy ignored the sign that looked like it was stolen off an aquarium and started rapping his knuckles against the glass. The others picked up his lead, except for one scrawny little boy, who pushed his mouth against the wall—there was always one of those. Sometimes the kids could get to you like a corset that had a broken piece of boning digging into your side. I took a breath and picked up my needle point.

Everyday, from eight until five in the afternoon, I pretend to be the character of sixteen-year-old Ellen Bloome, daughter of Mr. and Mrs. Isaac Bloome, and older sister to seven other children. None of them actually exists except the fictional month-old Belinda; one of my rotating tasks was to play with her in her crib. Another task was picking up the other children's scattered toys from the kitchen floor. I worked at a living history park.

My days were spent in the exhibit of a lower-middle-class 1890's kitchen with only Mrs. Bloome for company. For an eight-hour day my tasks as Ellen were:

- Play with baby: pointless—she didn't exist.
- Read: but only the period books provided.
- Clean up toys: pointless.
- Dust: pointless.
- Dry the dishes: pointless—they were never wet nor dirty.
- Be courted by James Lively, the store owner's oldest son, who, outside of the park, was already married.
- Work on my needle point.

Somebody thought this exhibit gave an accurate view of life in 1890.

My list of sanctioned activities was at least better than that of Mrs. Bloome. Restricted to cooking dinner and washing dishes, the boredom really got to her. Not only that, but there was no sense of pride when you spend the day stuffing a fake turkey with fake stuffing and putting it into an oven with no fire inside it. The exhibit went through a lot of Mrs. Bloomes every year.

I looked up from the final touches I was putting on a little brown cow that I was cross-stitching into my piece of linen to watch Mrs. Bloome mutter to herself. This sampler would be sold in the general store and forgotten about after it was brought home. It was the last sampler I would be making for the general store that day.

Mrs. Bloome slammed down a heavy cast-iron griddle onto the top of the oven. This current Mrs. Bloome used to go by the name of Mrs. Smith—the aptly named wife of a blacksmith. Why she had been given a change of roles—a demotion, to be sure—was one of the few mysteries of the park. There had been a fire at the blacksmith's shop, but the rumors about who started it had been vague. Usually word would spread despite the park's efforts to place us in corsets and behind glass walls. A kettle, on the only working burner on the oven top, started to scream.

"Ma?" I said, keeping in character so any visitors that paused outside our exhibit wouldn't have their illusion of the past stripped away.

"Mrs. Smith," she snapped, spinning around to glare at me.

At the blacksmith's shop she had painted roosters and cows and slogans like "Home Sweet Home" on decorative cast iron skillets that were sold in the general store in the same section as my samplers. The painted skillets were discontinued when she was demoted. Now she pretended to wash dishes.

The last Mrs. Bloome had been fired when the park discovered she had been making small batches of moonshine in the sink. The park never would have caught on if she hadn't sold a jarful to a bored eighth grader who got blitzed, did a dance in the gazebo, and then vomited up his lunch just when a crowd had gathered. For a time the park had banned the making of tea in the kitchen to make sure no potent brew was making its way into the tea cups, but they relented due to good behavior and we had our privilege back. Mrs. Bloome *nee* Mrs. Smith had yet, it seemed, to find a pastime besides banging pots and pans and ignoring tea kettles.

"I give her two weeks," Beth had said as we were walking to our cars the evening after Mrs. Smith had been demoted—almost four long weeks ago.

"Are you going to take that kettle off, Ma?"

With her towel she shoved the kettle onto the back burner, returning silence to the exhibit. While she rooted around in the cupboard for the loose tea, I went to Belinda's crib. My cotton petticoats were pasted down to my legs due to the heat and hardly rustled as I moved about the kitchen exhibit. I knelt next to Belinda's wooden crib that was empty except for soft blankets over a pillow to give the illusion of a baby—and my samplers. I put all the samplers that would make their way to my online store instead of the general store into the baby's crib out of view of the visitors that passed the exhibit. I retrieved from Belinda's crib the sampler that I had started the other day.

Between my daily chores, I spent my time making cross-stitch wall hangings of different sexual positions. The boredom got to all of us, but we found ways around the monotony and my way happened to pad my rather small paycheck when the hangings sold on eBay, or my store.

On the other side of the glass, James Lively was walking by with a package wrapped in brown paper—contraband from the 21st century for one of the live-in families. He saw me looking and tipped his hat. In high school I couldn't even get a date and now I have the older and sturdy-looking James Lively by my side, offering his arm, whenever I leave the kitchen. I smiled at him in return.

James dreamed of leaving our farming community and heading down south to fight in the Civil War every day until his throat became raw from the rebel yell. His wife, who worked at the high school—not in Wentworth—refused to leave. I often forgot that he had a wife even though I had met her once at a staff cookout. Most actors weren't history buffs like James. There were a lot of actors who spent all day in character and then donned another character at the theater so they never had to be themselves and could dream of Broadway.

Then there were those that were like me and Beth. There was Ms. Teresa Tomas who made baskets and led a two-hour workshop for school kids everyday. "Those kids," she'd say after a long week as we traveled to the parking lot in our jeans and summer tops, "are going to turn me into a basket case," and she would laugh the rest of the way to her car. In her purse she would have a collection of miniature baskets she would sell to dollhouse enthusiasts and a few ring boxes made from willow. The park never seemed to miss material that disappeared from different exhibits.

There was a time—before my figure drawing class at the community college—when I would sit in the straight back wooden chair carefully stitching the alphabet, farm animals, and words like *Congratulations* and *Welcome* into the linen stretched tight in my wooden hoop. My fingers became more nimble with needle and thread when they started to remember long days spent cross-stitching with my grandmother. Soon the slogans lost their challenge, plus I was making more samplers than the store could sell. I turned my needle and thread to other, more interesting, samplers.

Mrs. Bloome cursed the heat under her breath. I was forced, by my delicate 1890 glasses, to bend closer to my linen. I worked peach-colored thread into the form of a naked woman spread out on an invisible bed while a man in the same bland peach thread went down on her. I had the perfect stitch that comes only from hours practising every day. One miniscule stitch after the next formed the woman's face to make her the picture of boredom sprawled in incompetent hands.

This sampler was a special order from a disgruntled wife for her untalented husband's birthday. In the comment section of her order form, she had written a list of suggestions her husband might want to try that she requested stitched around the image. She had asked for a title to appear on the piece saying "It's an Art."

"Come get your tea," Mrs. Bloome said. She tossed spoons loaded with honey—also made on Wentworth farm—into the cups, making the tea splash over the side.

I sat my needle work facedown on the table and arranged the excess linen so it hid the image shown there. But it didn't matter, no one was outside our exhibit—something more exciting than two women drinking tea had to be happening in other parts of the park. "Do you think needle point will fit on a college application?" I asked after taking a sip and leaning against the counter as much as my corset would allow. I felt my body temperature climb as I wrapped my fingers around the mug and took another sip. I rested my other hand against my corset covered torso. I could feel the thin steel stays encircling me like a cage.

She looked at me, her sour face puckering more at the brow and around the eyes. "Can't say I know anything about college applications nowadays," she said. "Never thought I'd get a degree and work here."

I nodded my bonnet-covered head—nobody ever thought they would work at Wentworth. Working here is just something that happens. Nobody can say what step they took that directed them down the path of working as an exhibit.

Outside, a wagon with two dozen kids hanging helter skelter from the bed rumbled by on Main Street. The street led from the visitor's parking lot, through the center of the Village, and onto the barnyard of the dairy farm. I squinted against the sun to see the kids. Their private school clothing had turned brown with the dust from the road. The cookware on the shelf rattled as the wagon passed. The driver held the reins slack, letting the two Morgan horses weave like drunks up the road. Shrieks and whoops came from the kids with every pothole they crashed over. Beyond the wagon load I saw Henry—a tall lanky figure dressed in soiled overalls with no shirt. He was a farm hand who loved working with animals and he looked the essence of hick. And happened to be rather attractive at the start of the day before he started smelling like a barn.

"I heard you take drawing classes."

"Yeah," I said when the china stopped rattling in its grooves.

She snorted. "What do you think that's going to get you? Go to law school if you want to get somewhere."

I didn't answer. I could have told moonshine-making Mrs. Bloome about my needle point and the online store that made enough to pay for more courses, but not this Bloome.

"All of you," she said, jutting her chin at me and I knew she was talking about anyone young enough to go to college, "think that it's so easy to do something that matters."

I felt my spine bristle—and it wasn't a reaction to the trickle of sweat running down my back. "What did you do to get demoted?"

"Haven't you heard all the rumors? Didn't you hear the one about me hitting Mr. Smith over the head with one of the skillets?"

"I heard that one; it didn't sound very convincing." Mr. Smith was another one of those history enthusiasts and hadn't missed a day of work for ten years—as park gossip goes.

She shook her head, "Did you hear the one about the fire? Or are you too busy being the park pet, keeping to your tasks and never causing any problems?"

"I heard about that one, too." There had been a fire that had caused men to take up wooden buckets filled with water to try to douse the flame. One of the managers was alerted and came running. He broke the park's illusions by dragging a safety hose out of hiding and spraying down the forge. The place was hardly burnt—just a little smoky. "That one I believe. You seem like someone who would fail at a plan so simple."

She hacked out a laugh before she grabbed me by my corseted waist and tugged me close to her. My mug of tea leapt from my hands, spilling on my dress before the clay shattered on the floor. The toes of our lace-up boots touched and crunched the clay. I could smell her breath, tinged with chamomile and honey—nothing stronger.

A passing tour group had stopped outside our exhibit—their destination completely forgotten as Mrs. Bloome gave me a brisk shake, leaving me gasping for breath. "Do you think you're doing these kids any good by working here? None of us are. This place isn't a dairy farm. It's just a place for a bunch of misfits one paycheck away from welfare to dream about another life. Those kids out there," she said jerking her head towards the glass wall, "they're not learning shit. I don't want you to think otherwise."

"I know that." I had known that since first grade, when I'd been taken by the hand and led around Wentworth Village.

"This whole place should be burned down." Her eyes darted to the counter next to us so quickly I didn't think she had time to register anything upon the surface. One of her meaty hands released its grip upon me. "This whole place is a shame. It needs to be completely undone."

I heard buttons from my dress rolling away across the floor before I realized she had a knife in her hand. It sliced through the thin cotton of my dress and moved up snapping the laces of my corset. I saw the glint of the knife like a newly minted quarter as it came up towards me.

The cords that had always felt so sturdy in my hands every morning when I laced up, pulling tighter every day, cut as easily as my scissors could cut the thread for my cross-stitching. The blade moved so fast in Mrs. Bloome's hand that I didn't have time to try to get out of its way. I heard the last cord snap and felt the blade bite into the bottom of my chin—my bone halted its progression.

For the first time in a year I took a full breath.

I stumbled back into the table hard enough to send it rocking. I brought my hands to my face only dimly aware of the pounding on the glass wall. I moved backwards while keeping my hands pressed against my wound not taking my eyes off Mrs. Bloome. She seemed to forget I was there as she went about cutting her own dress and laces underneath. The knife left behind a tint of red.

The backdoor to the kitchen exhibit flew open—a gust of fresh summer air hit me as the door just barely avoided smacking me. The park managers —three dull-looking men wearing brown suits stained with sweat under the arms—crowded the room. Two of them made a beeline for Mrs. Bloome to take her down.

"Are you alright, Ellen?" said the other manager while putting a hand on my shoulder to steady me. His body blocked Mrs. Bloome from my sight. I thought he was a stupid man, turning his back on her like that; but then her voice dropped, and I heard the sound of metal against wood as someone put down the knife.

"I think so," I said even though my fingers couldn't contain the blood and my legs shook underneath me.

"Let's get you in a chair," he said and started to guide me towards the seat I spent most of my day in.

He pulled the chair out. Laying there was my sampler, but he hardly glanced at it as he picked it up and dropped it on the table. His eyes looked slightly unfocused and I could see he was thinking lawsuit.

Once I was sitting he crouched in front of me and put his hands on my wrists. "Let me see," he said. He gently moved my hands aside. "Not as bad as I thought," he said with a sigh of relief. He let go of my hands and stood. He was surveying the exhibit, clearly wondering how long it would take to clean up the blood, find a new Mrs. Bloome, and get the exhibit opened up.

I heard the voice of James coming through the glass wall, trying to dispel the crowd that was reluctant to leave.

The manager went to the oven and brought back the same dish cloth that Mrs. Bloome had used earlier to make tea. "Use this," he said handing it to me. "Dr. Horace will be here soon."

He wasn't looking at me or he would have seen the way my body jerked back as if another knife had been pulled on me. "Oh no," I said, "I don't need him." Grisly old Dr. Horace wasn't, of course, a real doctor.

On the table my sampler was laying fully exposed—the carefully arranged fabric no longer hiding anything after he had dumped it on the table. I reached one sticky hand towards it.

His head jerked towards the sampler as I reached for it. "What is this, Ellen?" he asked.

"It's-" what could I tell him? I could say it was porn or art or something I was just messing around with saying that I was bored. "It's a sampler, Sir," I said.

"I can see that." He reached out to pick it up and I could see his eyes move from the woman's body to the suggestions. "You have some explaining to do."

"If I could, I'd like to go to the hospital now."

"No need for that. Dr. Horace can stitch you up right quick. Or maybe you don't need him because you seem to have mastered the needle and thread."

"I took a figure drawing class. We had nude models come in and pose. And I was good at it—drawing the human form. The human form is art."

He looked again at the sampler. His eyes moved over the woman's body: the bored face, her breast, down to her cunt that was mostly obscured by the second figure's head. "And this is art?" he said holding it out for me to see.

I stuck my bloody chin out defiantly. "Yes. It's art."

He looked again, his eyes going over the title of the piece. "Yes, I suppose it is. Just don't make this type of art here anymore."

He put it down and left the exhibit with a faint blush upon his face. "I'm just going to go to the hospital now," I called after him. I stood, and reached a blood streaked hand in the gaping hole of my dress. From under the fabric I pulled my ruined corset. I let the corset drop to the floor. Its steel stays clattered against the wood floor. While attempting to hold the dish cloth to my chin I slithered out of my tattered dress and petticoats, stepping once or twice on the fallen corset in the process. The plain shift that I wore under the corset, which looked like a girl's nightgown, was still whole.

I picked up my sampler by the very edge of the linen. On my way out of the exhibit the shift skimmed my knees and my boots thudded across the floor. I paused by the cradle and from it I plucked the rest of my samplers from under the blanket, leaving behind a rust colored smear on the soft fabric. I would have to buy some thread on my way home from the hospital if I was to finish the piece in time for the mail.

n

Lyndall Henning   Tula

My little sister was born on a hot night in mid-summer. I remember this day clearly because it was the first time I saw a glimpse of what hell is like. Summers in the high veldts of South Africa are always very dry, but that evening, the inside of our little hut was as sticky and humid as a labourer's armpit.

My Auntie Tebogo chased me out when my mother's birth-pains began. The sun had only just been setting then, lighting the sky on fire. I sat on an old wooden crate and scuffed at the cracked, red earth with my bare foot. I was trying not to hear the muffled screams coming from inside. I watched as the sun slowly sunk over the horizon, becoming big and pinky-orange like a giant guava fruit before disappearing from my sight. After what seemed like hours, my mother's cries were suddenly joined by the pitiful, piercing screams of my new baby sister.

I waited then for my Grandmother or Auntie Tebogo to call me inside again, but no one came, and my mother's cries didn't stop. They became quieter and quieter and weaker and weaker and then they just faded away. I held my breath as I waited for them to start again. They *had* to start again, because if they didn't it meant…

There was an odd kind of lurching in my stomach that moved up to my head, as if I had been spinning and spinning in circles and then stopped suddenly. I didn't want her screaming to stop anymore. I wanted it to start again. I wanted it to be loud and throaty as it had been when she first went into labour.

By now the sky was completely black and starless. It seemed endless and so lonely. I wanted more than anything to be inside our hut. My heart began to beat fast and I could hear my Grandmother's and Aunt Tebogo's voices muffled and desperate inside.

The baby was still crying voice rising and falling, but never stopping, never needing to pause for air.

I couldn't stand it any more. I stood and pushed my way through the thick curtain of fabric that hung across our front doorway.

I remember my Grandmother once telling me about hell. She said it was the place where bad people go when they die. She said it was full of blood and fire and gnashing teeth. I was not sure what gnashing teeth were, but what I saw before me as I pushed back that curtain was how I will always picture hell.

There was blood everywhere—the floor, the mattress, even the walls seemed drenched. The oil lamp lit up my Auntie and Grandmother's faces from underneath so they looked dark red and skull-like in the flickering light. And in the centre of the bed lay my mother. I suddenly completely understood the meaning of the phrase 'dead still'. I had never seen anyone stiller in my life. Her chest seemed to have caved in on itself completely and she was smeared with blood all over.

That was the worst thing. The smell of blood—dark and metallic and animal. It hung heavily in the air and made me gag even as I tried to open my mouth to scream.

Auntie Tebogo staggered to her feet, reaching for me.

"Eh! Keletso! Please!—I'm sorry, girl—No wait!"

But I couldn't stare at that nightmare anymore. I turned and ran away through the dark, cluttered lanes of the squatter camp, unable to stop, and the baby's cry seemed to follow me through the streets. It was a tiny thread of a cry and it was stretched thinner and thinner the further I ran. I suddenly I had a terrible vision of it snapping, just as our mother's had, so I followed it back. I followed it back even though all I wanted to do was run forever.

They wouldn't name her—my Grandmother and my Auntie Tebogo. They said that she was tiny and weak and would probably die anyway. There was no point naming her because it would taunt God. They said it would be like screaming to him "She is ours! You can't have her! Look, she is a little person, not just a nameless baby!"

"Good!" I said to Auntie Tebogo, "She *is* ours. He *can't* have her."

Auntie Tebogo was shocked and hit me hard around the face so that my head went fuzzy.

"Do not talk like that!" she hissed at me as tears trickled from my eyes and ran down the side of my nose to slip in the corner of my mouth, "He will hear you and take her!"

And she rocked the baby, who cried all the time, waving her tiny, thin arms and legs and screwing her little black eyes shut in pain.

"*Tula, Tula mtwana,*" she sang gently. Hush, Hush my baby.

Auntie Tebogo has the same disease my mother had. No one likes to say its name, but nearly everyone I know seems to have it. You can see it squatting there like a shadow behind their eyes whispering the name like a curse. And these people who have it become thinner and thinner and they are always ill. They get sores on their skin, and eventually they die.

Aunt Tebogo has a hacking cough that tears up her throat so she coughs up bits of skin and blood. Her arms and forehead are covered in sores, and she is too weak to work. My Grandmother is old, but she goes out to clean the houses of the rich people so she can earn us some money to eat. I am left at home with Auntie Tebogo who just sits in the corner rocking the baby she won't name and singing "*Tula, tula,*" to try and stop her from crying.

One day, a white aid worker from England comes to our house. She looks at Auntie Tebogo and she can see the shadow behind her eyes and the sores on her skin. She has pale, reddish hair like the earth outside, and her eyes are as grey as summer storm clouds. Her skin is burnt and freckled from our African sun and her upper arms are round and plump and soft, reminding me of bread dough before it's cooked.

"We will look after you if you come to our shelter," she tells Auntie Tebogo, "We can take care of the children." She looks to me and then down at the baby who has no name. She speaks in English and her accent is strange.

"We can look after ourselves!" Auntie Tebogo says, also in English. I don't know why she is so angry.

"Our shelter is on Goldman Street. You know where that is, don't you?"

"*I said we will look after ourselves!*" Auntie Tebogo screams and then she starts coughing again, staggering up and waving her free arm at the aid worker as blood-tinted spittle clings to her lips and the baby with no name screams in protest.

The aid worker is afraid and leaves our hut. I see tears in her eyes as she goes and I wonder if she is crying in fear or because the sound of the baby with no name's endless crying is too sad to hear without crying herself. I know how she feels. Sometimes, when Auntie Tebogo falls asleep, I sneak the baby out of her grasp and rock her gently as she cries. I sing like Auntie Tebogo "*Tula, tula mtwana.*"

Once, a long time ago, before the baby was born and I wished more than anything for a little sister, I made myself a doll out of sticks and string. It was delicate and scratchy and threatened to fall apart when I held it. That is what I am reminded of when I rock the baby with no name.

The winter comes and Auntie Tebogo is worse. She can't get off the mattress now and the icy air of the high veldt makes the water turn to ice and our breaths turn to smoke in the air.

We huddle together on the mattress at night—my Grandmother closest to the front door that we have tried to barricade against the cold with cardboard boxes; then Auntie Tebogo; then the baby with no name; and last of all me. I sleep with my back to the corrugated iron of the back wall, and sometimes it gets so cold it actually seems to burn my back until I can't sleep from the pain.

I curl up around the baby with no name. I make my body into a nest for her so she is surrounded by my heat. I lie there breathing warmth onto her face as my back burns and aches with the cold, and Auntie Tebogo's laboured snores fill the air.

My Grandmother is getting too old to work now. She can't wake up in the mornings properly, and I have to kneel beside her and rub her legs and arms so she can begin to move them. I remember the same thing happening to my Grandfather a long time ago, and I am frightened, because I know that I am sitting there rubbing death from her limbs, and that one day I won't be able to do it any more. One day I will wake up and she will be cold and stiff and no amount of rubbing her arms and legs will cause them to move again.

We still need money, so now I go to a car park belonging to the big mall on the outskirts of town and direct the rich people into spaces. Most of them just yell at me to get out of the way, but some give me money so I can buy bread and mielie pap to keep us alive through winter. One kind lady gives me a coat so that when I stand out there, the cold doesn't cut into me quite so cruelly in the dry winter air.

I spend a lot of what I earn on milk for the baby, and new pieces of cloth for her nappies, but she seems to be getting thinner and thinner, and now she doesn't cry all the time. Sometimes she just lies in my arms and whimpers as if she no longer has the strength to cry. And like that time that seems so long ago when my mother's voice faded into the dark night, I wish she would cry again. Because then I would know that she was strong and alive.

"Can't we go to the aid workers in Goldman Street now?" I beg Auntie Tebogo when she is awake one morning and lying there shivering on the mattress.

"Never!" she snaps at me, her eyes shiny with pain, "You are a silly girl, Keletso! They are responsible for all this. We will not go and live off their charity!"

I don't understand what she means. I never remember seeing aid workers nearby when my father was shot on the farm where he worked. I never remember seeing aid workers nearby when the farmer threw our family off the farm because my father could no longer work for us. I never remember seeing aid workers around when my mother, Auntie Tebogo and I built out little hut out of any scraps we could find so that they could get work as cleaners in the city.

She falls asleep again, her eyes half closed with the whites showing under her lids, and a thin sheen of sweat on her forehead. The baby who still has no name begins to cry weakly beside her, so I pick her up and rock her, singing; "*Tula tu, tula mtwana, tula sana…*" Hush, hush, my baby.

The winter seems so much longer this year. We are now about two months in and neither my Grandmother or Auntie Tebogo can move from the bed. The nights are getting colder and the baby whimpers and cries because I have to take her out with me when I work in the car park. I tie her to my front with a blanket and try to keep her head out of the cold wind.

One night it is so cold that I cry as I lie curled around the baby with no name on the mattress. The cold moves from burning the skin of my back and penetrates even deeper until I'm sure I can feel it inside my bones. I hear Auntie's snores becoming less and less frequent and more and more laboured. I must have dozed off because when I wake again, her snores have stopped altogether.

The morning light is cold and ice-crystal blue from the clear sky outside. The wind has blown the cardboard away from the front door and the curtain that hangs from it flaps noisily.

I look towards Auntie Tebogo and I once again see that dead stillness that can only mean one thing. She is no longer breathing at all, and the arm that was pressed against mine as I slept is as cold as meat from a fridge.

I begin to sob then, because I no longer know what to do. I climb out of bed with the weakly stirring baby clung to my chest. I look towards my Grandmother, but even before I pull back the covers I know that there is not much point. She sleeps facing the front doorway, and the wind that whistles through. On a night as cold as the one just gone, no-one could survive.

The sky outside is so clear and blue and uncaring. I wish it were filled with storm clouds that would act as a blanket to keep a bit of warmth in for the world. I remember the lady with the eyes as grey as storm clouds and hair the rust colour of the earth.

The baby with no name wriggles against my chest and her little nose is icy with the cold. I don't think she has the strength to cry anymore.

I don't care what the aid workers did anymore. I don't care if they are responsible for what has happened to me. If they want to offer me food and warmth, then I will go to them. And I will take the baby with no name with me.

I tie her snugly to my chest with shaking fingers. I am still unable to stop sobbing and tears and mucus run down my cheeks as I gather everything from our hut that I can carry into the blanket that had been covering us on the mattress. I tie the top, then bend down to kiss my Grandmother and Auntie Tebogo goodbye. I wish I could bury them, but the ground is stone-hard and cold as dry-ice. I hope someone will take care of them once they realise they are dead—a grown up who knows what to do at times like this.

"I am sorry, Auntie," I whisper to her body, "But I can't take care of her on my own."

It is a long walk to Goldman Street in the cold morning air, but the thought of food and warmth at the other end keeps me going. When I arrive I see it is an ugly, concrete building covered with graffiti. There is an electric fence around the outside, and I don't know what to do. I stand before the gate staring in through the fence at the bright, warm rooms behind the windows. I see children in those rooms moving and laughing and eating.

Suddenly the front door opens and I see someone hurrying towards us down the path. My heart lifts in my chest as I see a flash of reddish hair emerge from her hood.

I can tell she doesn't recognise me because she looks at me kindly and questioningly.

"Can I come and stay here?" I ask her in English, tears beginning to run again down my cold cheeks, "My Grandmother and my Auntie Tebogo are dead and I have nowhere else to go."

"Of course, love," she says, and types a code into the gate so it swings open for me, "That's what we are here for—to look after children like you."

I consider telling her that I am not a child anymore. I don't feel like a child. But I say nothing because I want her to take us in. Otherwise my little sister will disappear, broken and hopeless like the tiny stick doll I once made.

"And who are you?" she asks as I follow her up the path towards the room beyond the front door.

The warmth of the entrance hall envelops us and the baby stirs in my arms, her tiny cry echoing round the entrance hall with renewed vigour and I whisper again, "*Tula, tula, mtwana...*" Hush, hush my baby.

"Who are you?" the aid worker asks again, looking down at us with a funny kind of sadness in her cloud-grey eyes.

I think of Auntie Tebogo with sores on her body and a thick sheen of sweat on her forehead. I think of the shadow that crouched behind her eyes to whisper the name of the disease to everyone who saw it. I think of my Grandmother, who could no longer have death rubbed away from her limbs. I think of them dying cold and filled with pain in our tiny hut because they wouldn't go to the aid workers.

But now we are here—in a warm room with electric light, not a hut with a back wall that burns my back with the cold and a curtain that flaps in the doorway. I got all this myself—for me and my little sister.

The aid worker waits patiently as I sniff and choke and look around the room with a mixture of terror and wonder. Eventually, I look up at her again and she raises her eyebrows in question.

"I can give her things now," I whisper to her.

I remember Auntie Tebogo sitting with my baby sister on her lap singing over and over again; "*Tula, Tula.*" Hush, hush. And the baby would sometimes recognise the repetitive, comforting words and calm a little.

She nods, still waiting for an answer to her question.

"I am Keletso," I tell her, feeling my voice fill with more certainty as I speak. "And this is my little sister. Her name is Tula."

Early Saturday morning, a small crowd gathered to witness a disturbance in the shopping precinct. Ryan Morne, nine years of age, moved a little closer to his mother. He wished he could hold her hand the way Dennis, his five-year-old brother, was doing.

Outside Fitzpatrick the Bookmakers, two policemen were struggling to contain a man who was scruffily dressed, with wild, matted black hair and a long beard.

"I am the Son of God, here to show you the way," the man screamed. "Turn from this sinful place and back towards the Almighty and you will be received in the Kingdom of Heaven."

Barry Fitzpatrick appeared in the doorway of his premises: "Get that mad man away from my place, officers. I don't want the Son of God telling my punters the winners. I'll be the poorest bookie in Ireland."

Many of the crowd laughed along with Barry, who Ryan knew to be a great man because Uncle Patrick had said so. He was a little confused about this, though, as his mother said that Barry was the man who took away all Uncle Patrick's money.

The policemen finally dragged the crazed man into the back of their car and drove away. Within seconds the crowd had dispersed as if nothing had happened and Ryan's mother placed a hand on his back to hurry him along.

"Was that man the Son of God, Mam?" Dennis asked.

"Don't be stupid, Dennis, he was only a nutter," said Ryan.

Their mother pulled them up short and dropped to her haunches. Ryan could see she was angry.

"Ryan Morne, never say that about anyone again. The poor unfortunate soul needs our pity not our ridicule, do you hear me?"

Ryan hated it when his mother thought badly of him.

"Yes Mam, I'm sorry… but he wasn't the Son of God, was he?"

His mother had calmed down; she never stayed angry for long.

"Well, now son, who can say. Nobody believed Jesus when he was here. Anyone could be the Second Coming, I'm not certain that even Jesus himself knew until he was an adult."

"Does that mean me or Ryan could be Jesus?" said Dennis.

Their mother straightened herself and this time grabbed both of them by the hand.

"We'll talk about this later. Right now, I think it's time for bacon sandwiches at the café, don't you boys?"

Dennis yelled his approval, but Ryan hadn't heard his mother. Dragged along by her forward movement, he was thinking about what she had said. Was it true? Could anyone be Jesus?

They arrived home from their shopping trip around mid-day and were met in the driveway by their white mongrel dog, Casper, who barked loudly and made it difficult for Ryan's mother to enter the house with the shopping.

"I wish John wouldn't leave that side gate open all the time. He knows this dog will be waiting for us coming home."

Through the open side gate, Ryan could see the brother in question, firing his high-powered air rifle at some tin cans standing on the fence at the bottom of the garden. On the other side of that fence a railway embankment rose fifteen feet so there was little danger of him hitting someone. Not that this would have bothered John, Ryan thought; at fourteen years of age, his older brother didn't care much about anyone. In fact, in Ryan and Dennis' experience, their brother seemed to enjoy causing misery. The only person John feared was their father, who at that moment was helping to build a by-pass somewhere in England.

"Put a lead on that dog and take him for a walk, Ryan, while I put this shopping away," his mother said.

Ryan was only too pleased to get away from the house and further think about what his mother had said that morning. If it was true that anyone could be the next Jesus, he thought, why couldn't that someone be him? Ryan had always felt that bit special; that bit different from all his friends. His father had said he had never known a boy read so much and was certain that Ryan was destined for great things. That comment had earned him a dead leg from John for being their father's favourite.

He recalled the story of a young Jesus talking to wise men in a temple and how clever they thought him. This led Ryan to remember something from a few months ago when his mother sent him to fetch Uncle Patrick from the pub for Sunday lunch. It had been a sunny day and Uncle Patrick was sitting with his friends at one of the wooden benches outside The Happy Fiddler. They often sat there and Ryan loved to hear them talk over important things, like who was the greatest American president, or who has the best Army in the world. He knew they were wise men because he had heard his father say so. "I don't know how your brother and his cronies are able to sit in the pub everyday," he had said to Ryan's mother. "They are wiser men than me. I work everyday and I couldn't afford to do it."

He remembered that his mother hadn't answered his father so he guessed Uncle Patrick and his friends were wiser than she was as well. On this particular Sunday, Uncle Patrick had seen Ryan approaching and announced to his friends:

"Now here comes my nephew, and there isn't a smarter young man in the whole of Ireland. I bet he can give us the answer to today's question. Come here, young Ryan, and sit next to your favourite Uncle."

Ryan had felt very grown up sitting with the wise men.

"Now Ryan," Uncle Patrick said, "my friends and I were discussing what the greatest piece of engineering on the planet is. What do you think?"

Ryan remembered how the answer had come to him straight away from something he had read in one of his science books.

"The Human Skeleton," he said with confidence.

Uncle Patrick and his friends were stunned into silence, an unusual state for them. Ryan had worried for a second that he had said something stupid, until they clapped their hands and roared with approval.

"Didn't I tell you this was the wisest young man in Ireland? Of course the greatest piece of engineering would come from the greatest engineer of them all, God himself."

Uncle Patrick had been so pleased with his nephew that he had insisted on buying Ryan lemonade, along with another pint of Guinness for himself, before they went home for dinner. Ryan had sat drinking with the men, feeling an equal man of great thoughts.

Out of sheer joy at that memory, Ryan began to run. Excited, Casper ran ahead of him until they were running so fast that Ryan knew he was out of control. He could see himself running full speed into a builder's skip and let go of Casper's lead. Too late to stop himself tumbling over, though, he put out his hands to break his fall, which resulted in him grazing the skin off his palms. He sat up and looked at the two red patches in the centre of his upturned hands, then scrunched his eyes shut in an attempt to stop himself crying at the stinging pain. He felt a soothing wetness and opened his eyes to see Casper licking at his wounds. Ryan immediately felt better and got to his feet to return home. He twirled the lead around his fingers so as not to aggravate the skinned parts of his hands.

Home again, he passed through the still open side-gate and around the back of the house. Dennis was playing on an old rug with his toy soldiers and, at the bottom of the garden, John was still firing holes into the side of a tin can. He had his back to Ryan and the young boy hoped it would stay that way. He didn't like being around his older brother when his father was away.

"Mam's gone back down the shops because she's forgotten something."

Dennis hadn't spoken loudly but Ryan knew instinctively that John had heard him. He turned to see a rifle pointed in his direction.

"Come over here, creep. You'd better do as I say; this rifle is aimed right between your eyes,"

Ryan froze to the spot. Somewhere in the back of his mind, he knew John wasn't going to shoot him, even he wasn't that stupid; but he was still scared.

"Come over here, now!"

Ryan still couldn't move and he wondered what to do next. Casper appeared to sense his discomfort and began barking at John.

"You'd better shut that ugly mutt up, Ryan."

Ryan was surprised at how scared John sounded.

"I'm warning you."

John took a step forward and Casper ran at him. There was a loud crack from the rifle and Casper hit the ground. The three boys rushed to gather around the dog, which now lay very still.

It was Christmas Eve, over two years ago, and they were about to go to bed when Uncle Patrick walked in. Ryan remembered him swaying slightly as he stood in front of the two boys. He smiled that warm smile, which always reminded Ryan of his mother. Then from out of his coat pocket he produced a little white ball of fur and placed it on Dennis's lap.

"There you go boys, your Christmas present from Uncle Patrick. Now be sure to take good care of him."

Ryan could still hear the groan from his father sitting across the room, and the puppy may well have gone back with Uncle Patrick if Dennis, who had only just learnt to talk, hadn't said excitedly, "Casper... friendly ghost."

Their parent's hearts had melted and the little white ball of fur had become a member of the family.

It was a growing red patch on the side of Casper's white head that brought Ryan back to the present.

Dennis began to sob loudly.

Ryan had never felt such anger.

"You bastard, you bloody bastard!"

He started to hit John. His visibly shaken older brother took a second to realise what was happening. Then he dropped the gun and grabbed Ryan by both arms.

"It was an accident, all right. I didn't mean to kill the stupid dog. Tell anyone about this and I'll make you wish I had shot the both of you instead."

Neither boy said anything, unable to speak for sobbing. John ignored this and ran for the old rug that Dennis had been playing on. He wrapped Casper inside and lifted him to his chest.

"Now listen carefully. There's a builder's skip just around the corner where I can dump the body. Ryan, when Mam comes back you'll say that Casper ran away while you were out and I've gone looking for him. Is that clear?"

Again, the two boys said nothing.

"IS THAT CLEAR!"

Not knowing what else to do, Ryan nodded. Then John was gone.

Not long after, their mother returned and she could see immediately from their tear-stained faces that something was wrong.

"Whatever is the matter, boys?"

To protect his younger brother, Ryan went along with John's plan. Dennis, as he often did when he was upset, said nothing.

"Don't worry boys, John will find him, you'll see," their mother said.

She cuddled them in close and Ryan felt strangely reassured by her words.

Twenty minutes later, John came back claiming he had searched high and low but had found no sign of Casper. Their mother praised him for trying his best. John tried intimidating them with a cruel stare, but Ryan noticed his older brother unable to maintain eye contact with Dennis.

Ryan and Dennis went back out into the garden while John went up to his room; for all his bravado, he was still clearly shaken by what he had done.

Outside, the two boys sat in silence on the concrete where the old rug had been. Dennis once more began to play with his soldiers, while Ryan looked at his grazed hands and remembered Casper licking them. Then, for the first time since the shooting, Dennis spoke.

"I wish one of us was Jesus, like Mam said this morning, and then he could bring Casper back to life."

Ryan tried to think of how he would go about bringing Casper back to life.

As if reading his mind, Dennis said: "If one of us was Jesus, what do you think we would have to do?"

Ryan had no answer.

"Maybe we should pray?" said Dennis.

Dennis screwed his eyes shut and pressed his palms together so tight that Ryan could see the blood disappear from the skin where Dennis' hands touched. Despite his skinned palms, Ryan decided to do the same. He couldn't think of anything to say, but his Mother had said that God always knew what you where thinking anyway and so he just said PLEASE over and over in his mind. He opened his eyes to see the face of his young brother transformed by a beaming smile.

"Should we go now?" Dennis said.

"Go where?"

"To the skip and bring Casper home."

Ryan thought that if he and Dennis could see that Casper was truly
gone, then they could both stop thinking about bringing him back to life.

"Come on then," he said.

As they approached the skip, Ryan was beginning to think this wasn't such a good idea. He imagined seeing Casper lying among empty cement bags, covered in blood, and thought it might be too much for them both. He was so engrossed in horrible visions that he nearly jumped out of his skin when Dennis shouted:

"CASPER, CASPER, HERE BOY, COME HERE CASPER!"

Ryan wondered what Dennis was shouting at; still some yards from the skip, there was no sign of life. Then he stopped in his tracks as a piece of cement bag lifted up into the air above the skip and slowly drifted down onto the road.

"CASPER, HERE BOY; WE HAVE COME TO TAKE YOU HOME," Dennis shouted again.

Looking down at his brother, Ryan felt desperate. At the same time, carried along by Dennis' certainty, he couldn't stop himself hoping. His eyes moved to the skip once more and he almost dropped to his knees as Casper popped his head up and began to bark. The dog jumped down onto the road as the boys rushed forward to meet him. There was a huge collision as boy landed on top of dog landing on top of boy, amid a hullabaloo of barks and shouts of joy.

As they exploded through the back door of the house, their mother squealed her relief at the sight of Casper. She had been dreading the next few days if he hadn't been found. At all this noise, John had run down the stairs to see who was making all the commotion. His face drained of blood at the sight of a ghost in the room.

"But… but, I shot that dog. He's dead; I put him in the skip myself," he blurted.

"YOU DID WHAT?" Their mother shrieked.

Ryan wrapped his arms around Casper's neck and cuddled into him. A broad grin crossed the young boy's face at the thought of all the explaining John was going to have to do on their father's return. Dennis was on his knees, running a tiny hand over Casper's dusty fur and Ryan thought he suddenly appeared much older. He said something that Ryan didn't quite hear so he leaned forward in the hope that his younger brother would repeat himself.

"It worked," Dennis whispered.

Later that night, a crowded bar at The Happy Fiddler listened intently to Uncle Patrick's extraordinary tale.

"…So they asked me to walk the dog to the vet and get it checked over. Apparently, the bullet had gone in beside the ear, ricocheted off the side of the dog's skull and out the back of the ear. Knocked the animal clean unconscious, it did. I'm telling you, it's a miracle that dog isn't dead. An absolute miracle."

e

Comfort Food

I wake up this morning after the sun's up, which is a something of a triumph for me, seeing as I've been tossing and turning the last two nights, but what strikes me right away is the silence of the house. It's an old farmhouse and has its share of arthritic creaks and moans, but this morning, it seems everything's still. You know how sometimes a dream will come back to you just like that? Well, sitting there on the couch, with the sweet, cool smell of dew drifting off the front lawn and into the window, and the finches in the shrubs outside peeping at each other, and Godbeams pouring through the curtains onto the coffee table, just like it's a dream come rushing back, I realize it's because Jeffrey's not poking at me to get him the cereal or tell him it's okay if he watches cartoons. And I'll never tell Tammy this—I swear I'll go to my grave with this on my chest— but knowing he'd never again poke me awake before the alarm goes off, well, it feels to me like the first day of a long overdue vacation.

My first thought was to make myself a real breakfast, the kind you can read the newspaper over. And while I'm enjoying the coolness of the fridge on my chest, I move the milk out of the way and spot, way back where Jeffrey never could reach, the cardboard box with birthday candles taped to the lid, and it dawns on me. Today he would have been five.

Now what kind of a father does that make me, huh? Back when Tammy and me were newlyweds, we used to dream of having a family, and here I am feeling fine about having that snuffed out by some maniac behind the wheel, and feeling good about it, feeling *free* for Christ's sake? When I lay eyes on that cake box, I'll tell you, that feeling of freedom drains out of my chest and runs down my legs like dirty shower water, and soaks down into the seams in the linoleum, and it leaves this vacuum behind so strong and cavernous that I feel like my body might turn inside out any second.

So I start thinking of what'll happen if Tammy decides to pull herself out of bed for the first time in two days and walks down to the kitchen. I pull the cake out and set it down on the kitchen table. I stare at it for a long time, wondering whether I ought to dump it in the trash, but I know that's the wrong thing to do. I can just imagine her trudging down the stairs in an old beach cover-up, her eyes and nose rubbed raw with wads of tissue and oily ropes of blonde hair flying off her head like reeds by a pond. She'd be carrying a roll of toilet paper in case she got caught up in another crying spell, and she'd stagger into the kitchen, pour a cup of coffee, blow her nose, and when she steps on the pedal and the lid flips off the garbage pail, she'd see the little acrobats piped onto what was left of the cake, cracked in half from me dropping it in the bin, and she'd look up at me like I was a stranger. But if I leave the cake in the fridge, she'd come down and head to the icebox looking for milk for her coffee, and there, staring her right in the face, is a tombstone of sugar and lard with six candles taped to the lid, and she'd start moaning, "And one to grown on." I'd end up pulling her off the floor and carrying her to the couch, and when she got on her feet again, she'd run back up to the bedroom and I wouldn't see her 'til calling hours. So I don't see any choice but to leave it out on the table in plain sight.

I'm sitting at the table blowing on a cup of coffee when I hear the shower turn off upstairs, and a few minutes later, here comes Tammy sashaying out of the hall with a towel wrapped around her hair like a turban, wearing a pair of khaki short-shorts and her lacy purple tank top, and I feel like salt crystals are growing in that void in my chest, sharp and poking at my insides. She's been sleeping upstairs for two full days, since a few hours after the accident, baking behind the closed door and windows even though it's been in the eighties for two weeks straight, but now she's the spittin' image of coolness. Her face looks silky, not all bloated and pink, and she's wearing the most honest smile I've ever seen out of anybody. I go stock still, frozen as a lizard, like somehow, in my cut-off sweats and two-day-old t-shirt, I might blend into the cabinets and she won't even notice I'm there.

"Morning, honey," she chirps, and drapes an arm over my shoulder while she kisses me on the cheek. If she notices the cake, it doesn't faze her newfound composure in the least.

"Hey," I manage to mutter, trying to decide how much of this is on the level.

She's off pouring herself a cup of coffee, and when she opens the fridge, she gasps. "Wow, who brought all this food?" she says, flipping foil off trays of lasagna and fried chicken, pulled barbecue pork and mashed potatoes.

"Oh, we've had all kinds of visitors while you've been upstairs the last couple days," I say, not meaning it to be backhanded, but I think it comes out that way, and once it's out, I realize I don't really mind if it does, even though she cocks her head back on her neck and grimaces like she'd just bit into her tongue. "People've been dropping off trays of all kinds of stuff," I say. She closes the door and turns back to the table. "Comfort food, you know? Somebody's put some flowers out by the road, too."

"Well, that's awfully thoughtful," she says, which strikes me as funny, because I've been the one answering the door a dozen times a day. I've gotten to the point where the bell rings, and I'm wearing my long-faced bereavement face on well before I grab the doorknob. And I swear, I've only recognized two or three of these people. Everybody's asks, "How's Tammy holding up?" while they suck on their bottom lip and hold their eyebrows up real high, and I tell them all, "It's rough, but she's surviving. We both are," when I really want to slam the door in their faces. Because what I'd rather be doing is sitting on the couch or the back patio with Tammy, spending time with her like we did before Jeffrey was born, just the two of us, because back then, we both knew everything would work out okay no matter what happened.

She sits down at the table and unwraps the towel from her head and lays it across the back of another chair, then starts scratching her scalp while she stretches so far over the back of the chair I worry she'll tip over. Her nipples are poking through her tank top, which is damp from her hair and sticking to her chest, and for some reason, checking her out feels like something I might get slapped for.

The cake's sitting between us like a centerpiece, the kind that always seems like it's in the way of conversation. I get the sense that's a problem, so I reach across the Formica, meaning to slide it off to the side, but she's reaching forward same time I am, and she's pulling it toward her. I sit back down and lean forward, waiting for her to stare at the acrobats and read "Happy Fifth Jeffrey!" aloud, and that's when I figure the outburst ought to start.

But she takes her spoon from her coffee cup and uses it to dig a chunk of chocolate icing off the side of the cake. She's sitting there, all prim and proper, back straight as a yardstick now—she's even jutting her pinky out away from her spoon as she dips into the cake a second time, flips the spoon over so the chocolate hits her tongue first, and closes her eyes like a TV chef and moans, "Mmmm," like she used to when I'd kiss her neck.

"You know," I say without realizing I'm going to. "You're looking awful put-together all of a sudden. What's the deal? Why the sudden change of heart?"

She looks me up and down my face, down to my hands, which feel, all of a sudden, like they could stand to meet up with a bar of Lava, and says to me, calm and measured as can be, "I guess I needed some time to let it sink in," and digs out another chunk of cake. "God, this is delicious. There's raspberry between the layers."

"I don't suppose a birthday cake for your dead birthday boy's the kind of thing that you'd freeze for later, like the top layer of a wedding cake," I say, and her eyes get wide. "But don't you think you're being awful... casual about everything this morning?"

She sets down her spoon next to her mug and glares at me, and I realize how with her hair wet, it looks more brunette than blonde, and it occurs to me she doesn't look much at all like the woman she was when we first started dating, or even got married, and all she's done is rinse two days of sleep and grief off her body.

"I want to look presentable today, Robert," she growls. "Maybe it's something you ought to think about."

But before I think of something snappy to say on my own behalf, I hear the doorbell ring, and as much as I want to get the last word, I know she's weaseled me into a corner. I stand up so quick my chair slides back against the Tupperware cabinet. "I'll get it. Wouldn't want you to have to leave your cake," I say. I've already got my bereavement face on.

Barb

I'm standing there on the porch in a clown suit, and the fellow that answers the door looks at me like I'd already tracked dog shit all through his house. Thinking I've got the wrong place, I glance over to the name on the doorbell. Tackett, it says, and I feel a little better, since I at least have the name right. Tammy I know in passing, but Robert's a stranger to me. The man standing there is in a yellowed undershirt and jogging shorts and looks like he's on the tail end of a three-day whiskey bender. I can't imagine Tammy bringing him home to her mother, but still, I go into my act. I toot my bike horn at the fellow—*honk-a, honk-a*—and do my little clown hop, where I jump straight up in the air and come down hard on one foot first, because it works so well on front porches; the huge clown shoes I wear thump the floorboards like a drum. Then I put my hands on my hips and throw a little sass at him and squeak, all sing-songy, "Where's the birthday boy?"

Kids love it when you sing a bit, and usually the parents play right along, since they're paying me to be there in the first place, but this guy doesn't say a thing, nothing at all, and he's not even smiling, but I can see he's grinding his teeth. His jaw muscles are blowing out the sides of his cheek, thumping like a heartbeat, and his eyebrows are squeezed together, and so I figure I've got to break the ice. I've got plenty of pockets sewn into my red pair of clown pants, so I pull out two balloons. I get them both filled with a single breath, and twist the red one into a circle and arch the yellow one over its top, twisted so there is a little spur of yellow coming off the front like a feather, and I step toward the man at the door and plunk it on his head. "Aw, come on, mister. Why so sour?" I squeak.

He just keeps eyeballing me, then I see him glance over my right shoulder out toward my car, which I'd parked on the side of the road so I could be sure I could take off when my three hours were up.

He looks like he's liable to break out weeping, and as a reflex, I guess, I start trying to look concerned beneath my makeup. "Mister," I say, using my regular voice now, of course, "do I got the right house? Birthday party? For Jeffrey?" I hold my breath, praying he'll say no, but then Tammy appears behind him, and I let the breath out, knowing whatever's going on is something even a clown can't fix. She puts her hand on his shoulder real soft, but he wrenches himself around like a drunk in a bar itching to fight, and I think he might take a swing at her, maybe. He doesn't, but he snaps, "I thought your mom was going to cancel all this fucking shit." She stares him down and growls, "Don't," and he lets out a yelp, turns, and disappears behind the door. I hear balloons squeaking and what I assume is him kicking a piece of heavy furniture.

"Won't you come in, Barb?" Tammy says and steps aside, sweeping her arm to the side like she's English royalty or something. Got her hair pulled back and brushed smooth, and she's wearing cute little khaki shorts and a tank top with lace trim that's a deep purple, the color of cherries. She looks together, not at all like her husband. This is a good sign, I figure, and hop right back into character.

"Gee, thanks, lady," I squeal, but she sucks her teeth.

"Barb, maybe you better quit it with the clown act," she says, which sideswipes me a bit, because how are you supposed to drop the clown act when you've got on the wig and makeup and you're swathed head-to-toe in red polka dots? You just can't do it, is all, but I go back to my regular voice, still thinking it's some kind of family spat.

"Where is everybody? Am I early?" But when I walk inside, I know I've walked into something awful. It smells like a locker room, like it's been all sealed up in this heat, and there's a sheet crumpled up in the corner of the couch, and a couple pillows with cases that don't match the sheets, so I know somebody's been sleeping out here. The hat I'd made Robert is sitting on an end table near the couch, so I figure it is a big bust-up between the two of them. But more than the smell and more than the disarray of the place, it's dead quiet, except for the fans. So I know then there won't be a party, and I figure it's okay to talk frank with Tammy. "What's going on?" I ask, but I'm thinking, "If the party's off, I'm keeping the deposit," not that I want to. It's just business, right? Which makes me feel awful when I hear what she says next.

She puts her palm on her forehead, then uses the back of it to wipe sweat off her brow. "Oh, Jesus, Barb, you haven't heard." She takes a big deep breath, and gets all this out in one exhale:

"Barb, the party's off. There was an accident, a car accident, and Jeffrey, he's, well, he's gone."

Now me being the dumb shit that I am, I think she means gone like in the hospital, so I gasp and put my hand on my chest and say, "Lord, Tammy, is he okay? Where is he?" Tammy looks over my shoulder, back toward the kitchen, and I look too. Robert's sitting at the kitchen table, pushed too far back from the table for anyone to sit comfortably, leaning forward with his chin nested in his crossed arms like a drunk at last call. The pits of his shirt really are crusted and yellow, and I can't be sure, but I think he's biting his forearm. He's bouncing his legs up and down on the balls of his feet.

She whispers to me, real soft, real, well, I guess motherly is the best way to put it, and says, "No, Barb, he's not. He's gone. *Gone* gone. Mom was supposed to cancel the birthday vendors, and we weren't expec—" Her lip gets to quivering, and she covers her mouth with both hands.

All of a sudden I'm awfully aware of my makeup and outfit, and I want nothing more than to slink back out the door I'd come in through and disappear. I think to cross myself, and I bow my head for a second and say a prayer. Not for Jeffrey, which would have been the right thing to do, but for help getting out of the house. When I open my eyes, Tammy's wiping her nose with her knuckle and Robert's up from his chair and glaring at me.

"Lord, Robert, I'm so sorry," I say. "Really, I am. It's just that nobody—" But he doesn't want to hear my excuse, so I figure the only way to save face is to walk out with my head up, and right now. "I'm awful sorry to have interrupted you two," I say, turning back and forth to look at each of them like I'm watching a tennis match, and I tell them I'll leave them alone and that they'll be in my prayers, and what she says next seems to really get under Robert's skin. He glares at Tammy from his nest of arms, not even bothering to pick up his head.

She says, "No, Barb, stick around. We're having some of Jeffrey's cake." She puts her arm through mine like I was her prom date and starts leading me toward the kitchen, but I stand firm and tell her I've got to be going. She says, "Come on, Barb. It's his birthday, and he wanted a clown." Now, she doesn't say it with the slightest hint of malice. Hell, she's smiling while she says it. So I can't very well argue with that, can I?

So we sit down at the table, me across from Robert, and Tammy pulls her chair up next to him, so I'm opposite the two of them, like it's a job interview or something. He's still got his chin down, but I don't realize until she's sitting next to him how put-together she's coming off. Her hair looks darker, almost the color of peanut butter, but that's only because it's wet from a shower—There's a white towel draped over the back of the fourth kitchen chair—and the hair is down on her shoulders, soaking her t-shirt, which must feel wonderful, because clown suits don't exactly breathe in this heat. Tammy's skin's not lost any of its youthfulness; in fact, it looks tighter and ruddier than I've ever seen it, while Robert, he looks a good fifteen years older than her, and I know they graduated together from Huntington High. The breeze from the window feels great on my scalp, but it is blowing over Robert and I can tell that locker room smell was his doing. He's got a beard growing, but not much of one. It's just a few days worth, not long enough to be even, and I notice the hair on the sides of his neck grows in peculiar swirls. But still I sit down and, thinking I'd try to be respectable, pull my red wig off and hang it on the back of my chair, leaving my white hair pulled back and slicked to my scalp under a hairnet. I regret it immediately; Robert looks me in the face and shoots me a look of disgust that's meant to knock me back on the floor.

"Cut Barb a piece of cake, would you?" Tammy says to Robert, and gives him a little playful poke with her elbow. She looks at me and smiles, and Robert uses the handle of a spoon to slice a wedge off a little chocolate cake that's sitting on the table and lets it tip over onto a plate, but his face stays still as a statue.

"Robert, you remember Barb, don't you?" Tammy says. "She lives down the street from Mom?"

103

He picks his head up from the table, finally, and sits back in his chair and stretches his arms up high, then laces his fingers behind his head, taking on the posture of a big-shot executive negotiating, like he's waiting for me to say something.

"Mr. Tackett, I'm—well, I'm awfully sorry to have disturbed you today," I start, trying to soothe him a bit. "To be honest, I was worried more that I'd be late for the party. With this heat, you know, I've got to use grease paint so I don't sweat it off, and it took a little longer than I'd expected it might."

Tammy looks down at her hands in her lap like she's mad at them, and like a snake uncoiling, Robert's up. He knocks the chair to the floor as he stands, and he storms past me, and as he passes the end table by the couch, he snatches up the balloon hat. He tears it in half, and cool as Tammy seems, she jumps out of her skin when it pops.

Tammy

I'm walking with Barb to sit on the couch, when out of nowhere, a Nerf football damn near takes my head off, spins end-over-end past me, and I hear a crash as it slams into the wall. I spin around, and there's Robert standing in the formal dining room, surrounded by Tonka trucks and Hot Wheels tracks, looking like an impish little boy. I stand back up and swing my arms up toward him, like an uppercut, and scream, "What the fuck are you doing?" but he doesn't say anything, just steps forward into the archway between the dining room and kitchen. He straightens his arms out to the side and presses his fists into the side of the archway and holds himself up that way, like he's Christ on the cross. His face is pinched up, and he even lets his chin drop down to his chin, and he's breathing heavy, like a thoroughbred after you run him too hard.

I look over to Barb. It's got to be tough to look terrified in a clown suit, but she is doing a hell of a job. Chewing her bottom lip and arching her eyebrows, even if I can't see them under all the white grease paint, and I feel my arms go tense and my face hot, because what kind of a goddamned piece of shit acts like this in front of company? If Jeffrey had pulled a stunt like that, I'd have sent him to his room for the rest of the day and whooped his ass when the company left, and I'll be damned if I was going to let Robert get away with it too.

"You see what he did, Barb?" I holler, pacing between her and Robert.

"Snuck back down the stairs and stalked me. Stalked me like an animal. Snuck around through the dining room and waited for his chance to kick a football at me." I turn toward Robert. "It's a hell of a way to show grief, you fuck." I stop pacing when Barb is between me and Robert. Spitting venom at him is easy. I want her to see what a child he is, and I want him to know she's seeing it.

Barb's looking down at her shoes, big as tennis rackets and the color of fire engines, and I hear her mutter, just above her breath, "I'd like to go now." She lifts her eyes just enough to peek at Robert, then at me, and I think, if you're going to look to him first for permission, you're sure as hell staying.

"No, Barb, I'd like you to stay," I say, and I cross my arms and hold my chin up like a bouncer at a dive bar. "I want you to see how much of a toddler he is."

"No, Tammy," he says, lifting his head and twisting it on his neck a little, thrusting a glare at me like a sword. "I think it'd be fine if Bubbles here skedaddled."

"I think I'm going to—" Barb starts, but I slice my hand through the air, and she stops.

"Stay, Barb. Please," I say, looking straight at Robert like I'm trying to push the evil eye back into his forehead. "You see how he is," I say. Robert's still hanging there in the archway on his own little cross. And then it hits me, how I can finish him off. "Look at him breathing like that, Barb. He's capable of anything when he gets like this," I say to her, and I touch my cheek just below my left eye. Even though Robert's never laid a finger on me, Barb doesn't know that, and I know I've won.

Robert bolts up, dropping his fists to his sides, then, like he thinks better of it, relaxes his hands. Then the red in his face drains, like he'd opened a spigot deep inside of him, and his face goes pale, and I think of how Jeffrey looked just after he'd stopped breathing, with all that blood in the grass and on my pants, because all that heaving breath that Robert had been blowing stopped completely. It's not that he's holding his breath. He just wasn't breathing, like it didn't occur to him, and I close my eyes for a second, because I feel like the ugliest bitch in the world. When I open my eyes, he's looking at me, his face almost blue now, and he turns toward Barb, who looks like she's trying to pull her eyeballs back into her head, she's so taken aback, and Robert says to her, "I have never once—" he says, but he doesn't say anything else, and the room is silent but for the fan humming above us and some cars buzzing past on the highway. He looks old, all of a sudden, like he's put on ten years this morning, and when he steps forward, Barb flinches so bad she drops her red wig. But he turns toward the kitchen, shuffling his feet like Dad did after his stroke, and my impulse is to rush into the kitchen and hang my arms around his neck, and if he doesn't look at me, to let my arms slide down his body like a fireman's pole until I'm on my knees begging him to forgive me.

When he gets to the fridge, I'm still standing near Barb, arms crossed over my chest, and I don't say anything as he opens the fridge and pulls out a plate covered in foil. He plucks the foil off and sets it on the counter while he gets a fork out of the drawer. He turns toward the garage, and I say, quietly, like he's right next to me, "Robert—" I say, but he doesn't hear me, and when he walks out the door to the garage, he stumbles on the threshold.

It's silent in the room for a moment—I don't even hear the rush of cars, and the fans seemed to have disappeared, because the water in my hair feels hot against my neck. Barb and I stand silently, like we're hearing a eulogy, until she says quietly, almost in a whisper, "Jesus, Tammy."

And I know, I know, okay? What a horrendous person I am, hitting below the belt like that, but he put me into that situation when he kicked the football, and I did what I had to do. Even if I hate myself for it, it still had to be done, or Robert would keep acting like this until somebody else did, a foreman at the plant, maybe, or a cop, God forbid. And I don't say anything to Barb, because what is there to say, after all this, until she says, "Tammy?" and I have to look up at her, for a moment hoping her makeup's shifted into the face of a sad clown, but there it is, that huge painted smile, and I know tonight that she'll call Mom, or maybe stop by her place, and when this gets out, Christ help me.

"Has he ever—"

I can't even bring myself to say no, that he's never once hit me, or that until a couple months ago, we hardly fought. Or how he tried, Jesus, he tried so hard to be a father, but his died before he was born, and he loved Jeffrey, but in a way only Robert understood. I can't say any of this. I just shake my head "no".

"That is some evil shi—" she says, but throws up her hand and huffs out a laugh. When I hear the front door close behind her, I'm still standing there in the middle of the room, all alone.

Jean:	Aged 60, married to Charles, timid, middle class.
Charles:	Aged 66, married to Jean, boisterous, posh accent.
Fossy:	Aged 45, neighbour, American accent.
Tom:	Aged 55, art tutor, shy.
Vicar:	Aged 60, camp.
Street artist:	Male, French accent.
Loudspeaker:	Male, West Country accent.

Scene 1

Interior – at a life drawing class

(Sound of chatter, pencils being sharpened, paper rustling)

Tom: *(Clears throat nervously)* I see we have a lot of new ladies here tonight. Super that word has spread about these art classes...

Fossy: *(Close)* Think someone should tell him it's not his teaching word's spread about…?

Jean: *(Close)* Fossy! I feel like a dirty old lady sat here. That model's very young looking.

Fossy: *(Close)* Mmmmmmm. What's that handsome husband of yours up to tonight?

Jean: *(Close)* Who? Charles? He's busy making his scarecrow for the fête. He's doing a model of the vicar this year.

Fossy: Talk of the devil…

(Door opens and vicar runs in rather flustered)

Vicar:	Apologies, one of the choirboys let off a stink bomb during the six o'clock sermon. Mrs Churchill-Brown fainted and landed head first in the communion wine…
Fossy:	Any excuse—she was guzzling all the samples at the wine-tasting evening…
Tom:	Ah vicar, do find a seat.
Vicar:	Budge up girls.
Tom:	*(Clears throat)* Ok ladies… and vicar. Unfortunately our model last term had to retire due to, er, unforeseen circumstances with a pair of scissors. Do read the Health And Safety sheets you've been given… *(Rustles of paper) (Pause)* So this year, we have Georgio. If you'd like to disrobe…
	(Sound of appreciative mumuring)
Vicar:	*(To self)* Hallelujah…

Tom:	Just give an overall feel of the body. We'll concentrate on details later.
Fossy:	*(Close)* A man after my own heart.
Vicar:	*(Close)* This makes a change from brass rubbings.
Jean:	*(Close)* Oh he is nice isn't he?
Fossy:	*(Close)* He can model for me any day.
Jean:	*(Close)* Not the model. I mean the tutor, Tom.
Fossy:	*(Close)* Oh… I prefer my men a bit younger, like a good blusher—put a bit of colour in your cheeks…

Jean:	*(Close)* That reminds me, how was your date?
Fossy:	*(Close)* A cheap hair spray—stiff as a board one minute then all floppy the next. I've taken my name off that dating agency. *(Pause)* I've discovered a whole new way to meet men… *(Loud whisper)* Internet chat rooms.
Jean:	*(Close)* Aren't they supposed to be dangerous?
Fossy:	*(Close)* Oh I do hope so.
Tom:	How are we getting on?
Jean:	Hello Tom. I'm not sure about shading…
Fossy:	I'm having problems with measurements.
Tom:	Just hold your pencil up for measurements… Fossy – isn't it? Now Jean, you're doing very well, you have such talent…
Fossy:	But Tom, what happens if it's bigger than my pencil?
Vicar:	Oooh I say, all my Christmases come at once…
Tom:	Eh? Oh… er… *(Clears throat)* Georgio, I think perhaps you need to change position. Ok class, let's have a break. Jean, can I have a word. *(Pause) (Close)* How are you Jean, it's good to see you again. I thought I might have seen you over the summer… we got on so well in pottery class…
Jean:	*(Close)* I know but… I had a lot on. Charles and I visited our daughter in New Zealand and time just flew… I did think of you though…
Tom:	*(Close)* Look Jean, I'm organising a painting trip, will you come along? I thought Paris…

Jean:	*(Close)* Oh Tom, you know I'd love to but I don't know, Charles…
Tom:	*(Close)* Forget Charles, come away with me, I want to get to know you better.
Jean:	Oh Tom…

Scene 2

Exterior – conversation over fence.

(Sound of pruning)

Fossy:	Hey honey, how's your roses?
Jean:	Oh hello dear, ruined in that wind. You've gone blonde! Have you got another date?
Fossy:	I've got a rendezvous with a web cam… It's great Jean. It means I can multi-date…
Charles:	*(Interrupting and breathless)* There's been a disaster —the vicar's head's blown orf!
Fossy:	Jeez, I told him not to re-wire the Vicarage himself.
Charles:	Blasted scarecrow. I've got to win that cup off the vicar this year. *(Pause)* Oh Fossy, you're looking rather lovely today. If I was ten years younger…
Fossy:	*(Giggles)* Steady, Charlie boy…
Charles:	*(Close)* Actually, this gives me a chance to re-design the vicar's ears. It's just not cricket Fossy, he wins every year with his scarecrows. Those spineless judges think they'll burn in hell if he doesn't…

Jean:	Charles, don't you think you're taking this rivalry a bit far. Just because the vicar's marrow was bigger than yours at the W.I. talk. I don't know what's got into you since you retired from the bank. I think you should take up…
Charles:	Only because he used fertiliser, whereas mine is totally organic.
Fossy:	Oooh, I love organic marrows… very tasty.
Charles:	Perhaps you'd like a nibble of mine one day, Fossy…?
Jean:	… an evening class—take your mind off things.
Charles:	I don't think that's a good idea, Jean. I still get twinges in my nether regions from that yoga class you sent me to.
Jean:	Charles got stuck in the lotus position. The whole class had to carry him into casualty still sat on his mat…
Fossy:	So that's why the vicar always calls you Aladdin.
Charles:	Yes well, *(Coughs)* we're doing Cinderella for the village panto this year. You should audition for the part of Cinders, Fossy.
Fossy:	Who's playing Prince Charming?
Charles:	I am of course.
Fossy:	My, we could waltz around the stage together, Charlie…
Jean:	That reminds me, I couldn't find any green tights in your size in Marks, so you'll have to make do with fishnets…

Charles:	Oh. *(Pause)* But did Prince Charming wear fishnets, Jean?
Fossy:	The best lover I ever had wore stockings under his suits.
Charles:	*(Coughs)* Get me two pairs, Jean. Well, must get on, check the vicar's not legless as well.
Jean:	Fancy some homemade nettle wine, Fossy? It's a new recipe for Charles's gout...

Scene 3

Interior – Jean's kitchen

(Cork popping on wine bottle and glasses being poured)

Fossy:	*(Spluttering)* It's very... tangy, Jean, and is that a caterpillar...?
Jean:	Oh, let me get it out for you...
Fossy:	Perhaps I'll leave the rest, I'm sure Charlie needs it more than me. You know, he's a sweetheart but I don't think I could put up with him.
Jean:	When you've been married forty years you get used to each other's ways.
Fossy:	I guess you're lucky. I've had lovers from all over the world and still not found "the one".

Jean:	I don't know that Charles was "the one" for me. We were in the cinema and I'd taken a huge mouthful of popcorn when he asked me to marry him. I started choking and he thought I said, "Yes please," but really I said, "I can't breathe." *(Pause)* By the time I came round his mother had made all the arrangements.
Fossy:	Oh honey, but you love him don't you?
Jean:	Of course. Well, *(Pause)* I think so. To be honest, I've found myself longing for something more just recently. *(Pause)* And I really like Tom.
Fossy:	Tom? *(Pause)* Our art teacher Tom? Oh my...
Jean:	He said he wants to get to know me better on the art trip—I don't know if I should be packing woolly jumpers for long walks... or borrowing your frilly knickers...
Fossy:	Oh you poor thing. *(Pause)* Go with the frillies, it is Paris after all...

Scene 4

Interior – Jean's lounge

(Children's art programme on TV in background. Hammer banging as Charles puts up a shelf)

Charles:	Pass me those nails, Jean.
Jean:	I'm trying to watch my programme. *(Pause)* Do we need another shelf?
Charles:	Of course, for the trophy. Not long now.

(Tap, tap, tap)

Jean:	Actually, I wanted to talk to you about that. I'm not going to be here for the fete.
Charles:	*(Bangs finger)* Ow! But Jean, you're rostered onto washing up duty.
Jean:	*(Sighs)* Look, there's something I need to tell you. I've been invited on an art trip. To Paris.
Charles:	Paris? Marvellous, I'll pack later.
Jean:	No Charles, I'm going alone. It's just for artists…and the vicar.
Charles:	But, who'll look after me?
Jean:	Fossy said she'd keep an eye on you.
Charles:	Fossy…? Did she now…?

Scene 5

Exterior – in a bustling Paris street

(Music – Charles Aznavour – Chanson d'amour)

Jean:	Oh Tom, it's beautiful here.
Tom:	Nothing is as beautiful as you. I've longed for this moment Jean, to have you to myself and tell you…
Vicar:	Ah, Bonjourno mon petit pals. Been looking for you two.
Jean:	Vicar. Love the beret! How was the Cathedral?

Vicar:	Oh, I got a bit distracted with the famous back passages of Paris.
	(Jean's mobile rings – we hear one-sided conversation with Charles)
Jean:	Charles? Is that you? Is everything ok?
Tom:	*(Close)* Look, vicar, can I talk to you man to man…?
Vicar:	*(Close)* Tom, let me stop you there. I've just met a charming young man…
Jean:	What do you mean your pants have blocked up the dishwasher?
Tom:	No, no. It's me and Jean, we wanted some time alone…
Jean:	I don't have the plumber's number on me, Charles!
Vicar:	To discuss art eh? Don't worry about me, my date said he'd show me his Eiffel Tower. Au revoir.
Jean:	How much of a flood is there? Charles? Charles?
Tom:	Everything tickety boo, Jean?
Jean:	Apart from a small flood and shrunken underpants, yes, I think so.
Tom:	Have some more wine then we'll take a stroll along the Seine and see the street artists.

Scene 6

Interior – Charles's house

>（*On Radio - music playing Tom Jones 'Sex Bomb'. Charles is singing along*）

Charles: "*Sex bomb, sex bomb, you're my sex bomb, you can give it to me when I need to come along…*"

Flossy: *(Calling)* Hey there, Charlie boy…

>*(Charles stops singing and music cuts to salsa rhythms)*

Fossy: Who was that sexy guy in the overalls?

Charles: *(Breathless)* Ah Fossy. Just the plumber—I had a slight accident. *(Charles claps hands and rubs together)* Now, where shall we do it?

Flossy: Ooh, that's what I like about you older men, straight to the point and no messing.

Charles: Well, I'm a little pushed for time, as I said I'd fit Marjorie at number 36 in today too. Shall we go upstairs or…

Flossy: Let's just do it here Charles, on the kitchen floor

Charles: Right you are. Oh Flossy, I've longed for this moment, to take you in my arms and…

Flossy: That's it Charles, oops, be gentle with me, show me what you want me to do…

Charles: *(Panting)* Oh Flossy, I, ooh sorry, I can't seem… to find my… I'm a bit… out of practice…me and Jean haven't… for a long time now…Oh…Oh…Ohhhhhh.

(Pause)

Flossy:	Oh. *(Pause)* Is that it, Charles?
Charles:	Awwwww, my neck, the floor was still slippy. I think I need an ambulance...

Scene 7

Exterior – back in the bustling Paris street

Tom:	Look at the detail, every stroke, every caress a brush of love...
Jean:	*(Distracted)* Yes. Would you like a mint? You had the garlic snails didn't you?
Street artist:	Bonjour Madame, you like to sit for me? I paint pretty picture for your husband?
Jean:	He's not my husband.
Street artist:	Pardonnez moi, Mademoiselle, your lover then?
Jean:	Oh... no... *(SFX - knocks into artists easel)* Oh, sorry, pardon, sorry...
Tom:	Jean, are you ok?
Jean:	No. Maybe it's the wine from lunch, I just feel rather, queasy...
Tom:	Jean, there's something I want to ask you.
Jean:	Oh... don't kneel in the dog mess, Tom. In fact... why don't you stand up?

Tom:	Jean, you have brought such colour into my life. Before I met you, I was monotone.
Jean:	I've always preferred magnolia myself.
Tom:	Now my heart is filled with longing...
Jean:	Actually, I'm longing to spend a penny, or is it a euro here...
	(Dog starts yapping)
Tom:	You are my muse, my Mona Lisa...
Jean:	I'm not going in one of those silver loos and having the doors open on me, though.
	(Dog growls and then bites Tom)
Tom:	Ow, Jean, get him off me, save me, my love...
Jean:	Oh, for heavens sake Tom, will you get up, you're making a fool of yourself. I'm already married. *(Pause)* I think maybe this was a mistake.

Scene 8

Exterior – village playing field

(Music – brass band playing Floral Dance)

Loudspeaker:	Welcome to Higglesfield's Village Fête. Would all contestants for the Dream Boys Look-alike Competition collect their leather thongs, kindly donated by Briggs The Butcher "A Sausage for Every Occasion" from the Lucky Dip Stall.

Fossy:	Charles!
Charles:	*(Subdued)* Hello Fossy.
Fossy:	Have any of your vegetables won this year?
Charles:	I didn't enter any. Jean normally helps me polish them.
Fossy:	I could have done that for you, honey. Let's go and get a cup of tea. We can have one of Mrs Marsh's rock cakes too. I hear they get heavier every year.
Loudspeaker:	*(Sounding fed up)* Will the parents of a small child wearing an ice cream please come and collect him from the main stage *as soon as possible. (SFX – feedback from microphone)* The judges are about to announce the winner of this year's scarecrow competition. All entrants kindly make their way to the main stage.
Jean:	Well, go on, Charles, that's you.
Charles/Fossy:	Jean!
Fossy:	When did you get back?
Jean:	Couple of hours ago, why's your neck in a brace Charles? Tell me in a minute, they're waiting for you…
Charles:	But I didn't enter the scarecrow.
Jean:	Lucky I did it for you then, go on.

Vicar on loudspeaker:	As I have won this competition for…well…*(Clears throat)* several years, I thought it best if I hung up my pinking shears and let someone else have a snip. So this year, I have been asked to judge the competition. We have had some super entries, from the Queen *(Aside)* my favourite, to a scarecrow of someone called *(Clears throat again)* Jordan. Apparently an extra bale of straw was required for that one. Anyway, without further ado, and to show that vicars do have a sense of humour, I would like to announce the winner, Charles Rigglesworth, with his scarecrow of *(Coughs)* me.

(Claps and cheers)

Fossy:	*(As clapping continues and with Charles saying thank-you in background)* What brings you back home early?
Jean:	Him.
Fossy:	Who? You haven't brought Tom here have you?
Jean:	No. Charles. I still love him. He rang me with some disaster when I was away and I realised I need him as much as he needs me.
Fossy:	Oh. *(Pause)* There's something I need to tell you about me and Charlie…
Jean:	What is it, Fossy?
Charles:	Well, that was a bit of a surprise, hey? Me and the old grouch just shook hands. He said love was well and truly in the air in Paris…
Jean:	Hey? Ah… I can explain…

Fossy:	I'll see you... around... Jean...
Charles:	Yes, apparently our vicar met someone... he's moving to Paris!
Jean:	Oh, thank goodness...
Charles:	Jean?
Jean:	Oh, no, I didn't mean... anyway, Fossy said you had something to tell me... and why are you wearing that neck brace?
Charles:	Oh Jean, I should have known Fossy would never be as good as you...
Jean:	As good as me? Oh Charles, you didn't...?
Charles:	I'm sorry my dear. I tried to teach her to Rumba for the panto, but it just wasn't the same as when we used to and I slipped and jarred my neck. Do you remember, when we were first married...
Jean:	We danced every night together in the front room...
Charles:	I've missed you Jean, life's not the same without you around.
Jean:	And I missed you too.
	(Band starts playing a waltz)
Jean:	Shall we?
Charles:	If you're gentle with me...

P

We weren't giving in on this one. Not in the rain. Not when we'd already been driving all day. No matter how cute she was.

Lilly shrugged and sat back, but waited only a second before leaning forward again. She hovered there, behind me, face nestled close, breath cool and damp in my ear, and the rhythm of her breathing started things happening inside my body, the chemical reactions that go on between males and females. Kyle blew air sharply out his nose. I caught him roll his eyes before he turned away and put his attention out the window.

In the mirror Lilly smiled her trouble smile, and then calmly and seriously wrapped her hands around my face, interlocked her fingers tightly over my eyes, and held on.

I was instantly blind, which was bad 'cause I was driving, but it was worse than that. She wasn't just holding, she was squeezing, and the pressure over my eyes brought out something deep in me, something compressed and claustrophobic. One of her fingers stretched across the bridge of my nose, and the pressure hurt, but the pain was lost when the fear came up in me, primal, a sour taste I couldn't swallow away. In the midst of it all, I smelled her vanilla lotion, and her skin, some mix of soap and something sweeter, something that came from inside her, and part of me was just happy she was back.

Lilly didn't panic. Not when Kyle started screaming a list of profanities at her from the passenger seat, not when my instincts went exactly the wrong way, and I stomped down harder on the gas, giving the car an extra lurch of forward movement, not even when we clipped the first of the orange safety cones blocking off the far right lane.

I jerked the wheel hard to the left, then found the brake too sharply, sending the car spinning across all three, mercifully empty, lanes of traffic. I gave up then and lifted both feet off the pedals, and the car finally, gradually, cruised to a limping halt. I sighed and a shudder ran through me, glad it was the middle of the night and nothing had hit us. Yet.

I still couldn't see anything. I began to feel the certainty of approaching doom. I could feel it coming, a tractor trailer or a bus, and each second that went by I expected the crash that would kill us all, throwing writhing bodies and smoking wreckage all over the highway.

Then Lilly removed her hands and giggled. I jerked my head in all directions, then slumped back in my seat when I realized we were safe. We all looked at each other and no-one said anything. We had somehow ended up in the far right lane, past the cones, pointed off the highway. The giant plastic peach loomed in front of us, framed neatly in the windshield by the wipers, slapping back and forth to the quick rhythm of a Motown song.

The peach looked like an ass to me, perched atop its massive white pedestal, with that suggestive cleft parting its smooth roundness. Kyle leaned forward and snapped off the radio with a hard click.

Lilly opened her door and she was out, skipping and sliding her way across the muddy field, not concerned with the rain or anything. Kyle cut his eyes at me meaningfully, but I didn't say anything, just calmly pulled the rest of the way off the road and put the car in park.

It was dark in the car. The night was so overcast that the only light came from the occasional passing car, as their headlights cut a quick arc across the windshield, first shining in my eyes, then illuminating Kyle's face. All the light passed through water, the rain in the air, beading and running down the glass of the window. It left the car seeming green and dark like an aquarium, and something, some combination of the quality of light, and the wet earthy smell in the air, and the closeness of the cramped interior, made the car seem swollen, like a wooden room deep in the bowels of an ancient ship, where the walls close in a few more inches every year. There were probably no women on a ship like that, but somehow, I bet there were still problems between friends. There always are.

Kyle looked at me, but neither of us said anything. I opened my door.

"I'll be right back," I said.

"You've got to be kidding me."

"What?"

"You're going after her? Let's just go."

He drew out the last word in a high thin voice.

"We can't leave her."

"Why not?" he asked, with nothing in his voice to indicate he was kidding.

"Fuck you."

I slammed the door behind me. Lilly was almost at the peach, striding across the field. It was hard to pick her out, with the rain coming down so hard I had to stoop over like some horror movie hunchback. I braced my hands over my eyes like a visor and peered out from under them. Nothing was stopping her.

Kyle was mad about more than our narrow escape. He'd had a problem with Lilly ever since she and I started spending alone time together. Which used to be what Kyle and I did.

There was this empty grain silo across the street from his mom's house, behind a bent-down rusty barbed wire fence—part of the abandoned chicken farm that was scattered up and down their road. It was a scary climb in the dark, hanging off the welded steel rungs above a dark drop, but it was even scarier in the light, when you could see the dark patches of rust and the worse parts, where light came through.

We spent hours up there, chain smoking and talking about love and how desperate we were to find it, and how good we would treat the girl good enough to grant it. Better than all of the dicks we knew who constantly had girlfriends. Like Kyle's brother Matt. And, after all that, after I had told him so many times how I would treat the hypothetical girl that loved me, he really thought I would leave Lilly, my Lilly, in the rain?

I started to walk faster toward her, then broke into a lumbering half run, head down against the rain and wind. I wished I had brought the keys with me, just in case, but I wasn't going back to the car and debating with Kyle.

Lilly reached the peach before I even got close, and I worried about what she was going to do when she got there, but she just stopped and looked up at it. She didn't move after that, still didn't turn around to see if I was coming after her, and part of me admired that. She only turned when I got close enough for her to hear the splat, splat, splat of my feet through the mud over the sibilant hiss and sizzle of the rain, and when she heard me she smiled like she was expecting me, and when she did, everything was OK again, at least between us. I slowed back into a walk for the last few feet and she nodded up at the peach.

"I thought we could climb it," she said. "But there's no way."

I looked up at it for the first time. It was massive, fifty feet at least, and up close it didn't look like a peach or an ass. It looked like a huge plastic orange ball. It was actually less impressive up close. The size was dramatic, but there seemed to be no point.

It was almost embarrassing. Who built this thing? I assumed it was a commercial for the peaches grown locally, but it was alone in the middle of a field, without a farm or store anywhere in sight, and it didn't have anything written on it. So how effective could it be?

There didn't seem to be any way up to it. There were no stairs or anything, not even one of those maintenance ladders welded to the side. The peach sat atop this giant white pedestal like a golf ball on a tee, and maybe there were stairs inside that, but I couldn't see any way in. No obvious doors.

It seemed weird to build something that big with no way back to the top, but I couldn't think of any real reason you'd need to get back up there. There weren't any lights to change or anything. I guess they figured if they built a way up it they'd constantly have to pull drunk or lovesick teenagers off. Not worth the trouble.

Lilly stepped closer and I wrapped her up in my arms. Her t-shirt stuck to her skin. I slid my hands under it and rubbed her back. She was soaked and slightly shivering, even though it wasn't cold. She buried her face in my chest and rubbed it back and forth, then pulled back and looked up at me, wide-eyed, beautiful.

"Thanks for coming to get me," she said.

"No problem. I missed you."

"It means a lot," she said.

The horn honked out a long, bellowing blast. I looked that way, but I couldn't make out much in the rain.

R

In the glare of artificial light that fills the windowless strip club every Sunday morning, with Madonna's "Lucky Star" blaring—broken occasionally by static—from out on the floor, I found a tiny, bloody baby in the trashcan of the dancers' bathroom.

The room smelled like stale smoke and sweat and fruity lotion. I covered the thing with my used paper towel, carefully tucking it around its feet, knowing that the baby came from the world of last night, a world that doesn't exist on Sunday mornings when we dancers wear sweats and come in after church for pole-lessons from Glitter.

I stood looking at myself in the mirror, the bags under my brown eyes, greasy dark hair and too-tan skin. My hand was on the lid of the metal trashcan, which covered the damp paper towel, which covered the mucus and blood-smeared baby girl.

"Time to get to work, girls," Glitter said over Madonna on the loudspeaker. I wanted to puke, but trained my eyes at their reflection instead. I turned off the faucet, my heart beating hard, irrationally afraid the discarded child would suffocate in there with the towel over its mouth.

Glitter glared at me with forty-five-year-old eyes hovering over a twenty-five-year-old body as I mounted the glass stairs to the main stage. "Well, Natasha, you look like shit," she said, her face crinkling in spite of her efforts not to frown. "Honey, you didn't even work last night."

Later, she said, "Move slower, Natasha-baby. This ain't a race, and we are *not* firemen." Glitter pulled on my hips to make me stick out my ass more and added in her Georgian drawl, "This is about *sex*, not exercise."

Glitter wore her tiny silver shorts and skinny heels like something she never removed. She shimmied up and down the pole like she was flossing her legs. I wondered how many little babies she'd given birth to and then let die in bathrooms.

"Tasha—do ya mind if I call you that, Hon? I want you to really watch what I'm doin' with my ass as I come down. Do ya see how it gets *extra* tight, and my ankles are crossed right at the *top* of my Gucci's? That's the way you slow yourself down to *slide*—just like this; are ya watchin'?— to the stage, and then grind your hips *real* rhythmic—see?—'til *everyone* is watching you. We don't want you to make 'em all go soft seein' that cheek get scraped up when you slam your big ass on the stage like last time, do we?

She stood up and leaned over me, one huge, perpetually hard nipple an inch from my mouth and said softer, "And, Tasha, I will not be the one cleaning up your shit when it comes flyin' out, cause trust me, Baby, I've seen it before, and it ain't pretty."

I wiped her spittle off my chin and thought about Genie, a stripper with round green eyes that made her look like a porcelain doll, and gold bracelets on both arms that jingled as she danced or detangled her curly blond hair or smoked.

She and I were hired the same night, and before we went on stage, she stood behind me in the dressing room, smoked two cigarettes, and said, blowing the smoke out, "Aren't you nervous?"

I shook my head and tried not to breathe. "You'll be fine," I said, glancing at her shaking fingers.

Her eyes darted from my face to my reflection, and then back again. "Can I ask you something?"

I put my earrings in, dangly red ones in hoops of rhinestones. "Don't worry," I said, ignoring her question, wishing she'd leave me alone. "You look beautiful."

Genie blinked at me. "I'm just getting so fat."

Actually, she looked a little emaciated. Her elbows were dangerously sharp, her skin a little too see-through. "Genie," I said. "I'm sorry. I really hate smoke."

She put her cigarette out on the countertop. "But, am I showing yet?" she asked and turned so her stomach was in profile. A gold navel ring hung from a tiny mound. "You can't tell, can you?"

I shook my head *no* and watched her light-up again, feeling sick.

When the class was over, I snuck a peek in the trashcan, but the little girl was gone. The janitor had even cleaned the blood from around the toilet.

In Calais, cousins aged eleven and nine.
We ate peas and ham, rode bikes
back to our tent, tiptoed on baked grass
to cool in a swimming pool.

We swam full-stomached
in pink-salmon costumes until our curls drooped.
We dipped in sweat, flies, verruca-plasters,
toddler pee and chlorine –
the poolside chalked white.

A German man with a kaleidoscope eye
stalked our swim; you belly-flopped
from the diving board, he clapped.
He walked behind as we left the pool in giggles,
our faces blank with ignorance.

In a changing room we shared a towel
to dry our elbowed knees, lank arms.
A peephole eye glued us in.
Through the crack we watched that man
in the room next to ours –
cross-legged like lotus, touching himself.

When we peeked again his eye stared back
so close it made me jolt.
He dropped a franc for us to catch.
We bent down – gave him
an eyeful of our stream-lined bony bodies.
Our breast seams not yet stitched,
hands sliding on tiles to find more silver.

We ran back to the tent that afternoon,
our pockets full of coins –
unaware that this exchange of payment
was for secrets.

T

Melanie Datz　　　　Duck and Cover

Before my father died, we lived in the middle of nowhere without a TV; without radios; without other people; without so much as the local newspaper or a phone. Keeping us free from all outside influences, protecting us from materialism and commercial desires, was a point of pride for my father, and Mom believed Dad knew what he was talking about, because he was the one with the survival plans. He must have felt it would be easier for us to focus solely on survival if we weren't distracted by the outside world, so the discovery of TV our first night at Grandma and Grandpa's was a revelation. We gaped and turned their TV set on and off, spun the knobs around to change the channels, and watched the static on the empty UHF channels. We played with the rabbit ears and demanded to know how it worked, how there could be such things inside a wood and plastic box.

"Christ, Irene, what are they, idiots?" Grandpa asked, leaning forward in his recliner and swatting with a magazine at whoever was closest. "Hey! Stop it you, Ron or Ken or whoever you are. We're going to watch Lawrence Welk." And like some Fifties sitcom family, my siblings and I sat on the floor, mouths open, watching the tiny people sing and dance across the screen.

Two weeks at our grandparents' house turned us all into TV junkies. Once we settled into our new house, Mom was always scornful and derisive when she found us clustered around the TV after school.

"I can't believe the trash you kids are watching," she said almost every day, but she was just as bad; she'd stand behind us, commenting about programs, and hours would disappear. Mom became a news junkie, was mesmerized by the nightly display of catastrophes, and amazed by all she had missed in the middle of nowhere: Watergate, the fall of Saigon, the energy crisis. The Iranian takeover of the US embassy convinced her that being disconnected from the news was dangerous, and so, first thing every morning and last thing every night, she watched the news shows, local and national. Every day she read the paper front to back, even the comics page. A few years later when we got cable, she watched CNN for hours at a time before realizing that she was watching the same reports every half hour. I think Mom felt ashamed of how little attention she had paid to the outside world, and she swore she wouldn't be so uninformed ever again. After all, the outside world was where the intercontinental ballistic missiles with nuclear warheads were going to come from. Because of this new understanding of the need to stay in touch with the world, she always kept a news radio station on while she was at work, just in case.

One Tuesday afternoon in March, the first really nice day of the year, when people at work and kids at school sat looking out the windows just waiting for the day to end, President Reagan made an announcement on the radio. I was in seventh grade.

"My fellow Americans, I am pleased to tell you today that I've signed legislation which outlaws Russia forever. The bombing begins in five minutes."

My mother was at her desk at the Red Cross headquarters, with plans for dealing with a toxic gas leak spread out in front of her, and when she heard the President's announcement she remained calm. She stood, slung her purse over her shoulder, and walked away like she was going to the ladies room or the vending machines. She said nothing, just headed for the parking lot. Not speeding—but not exactly going the speed limit, either—she drove to the high school and picked up Ron, Sandy and Ken, then called the grade and junior high schools so Grace and I would be waiting for her.

"A family emergency," Mom told the secretaries, "but don't tell them that. I need to tell them."

My name was called over the loudspeaker during math class and Mrs. Price gave me a hall pass. In the office, the secretary considered me, trying to decipher the family emergency, and told me to wait in front of the school. "I hope everything is all right," she said, pausing to give me a chance to tell her something, "but be sure to have your mother call if you won't be in for a few days."

"Get in, Anna," Mom said when she pulled up in front of the school's glass doors. "We don't have much time." Her face was shining; she looked like she expected great things, like she believed in what she was doing with her whole heart and soul.

It didn't surprise me that my mother believed the President, that she didn't stop to consider whether or not this was real. She had believed in the inevitability of nuclear war since she was five and knew, just as surely as Christians know Christ will come again, that one day she would hear such an announcement on the radio. What puzzled her was why nobody else reacted: The Soviets would certainly retaliate once our missiles were launched, but civil defense sirens didn't sound; radio stations gave no warning of the coming danger; and when she got to our schools all the students remained at their desks, calmly working instead of ducking and covering. Nobody but the Greer family was bracing for an atomic blast, and Mom said nothing. It's not that my mother lacked charity, pity, or kindness, but she believed in survival. In a situation like the one she thought we were facing, survival meant sacrificing others.

She didn't even call Grandma and Grandpa.

I wasn't told a nuclear attack was imminent. I guessed. Nothing else could have made Mom look so radiant, and nothing else would have caused her to play hooky from work and pull us from school. With all of us in the car, she sped through the suburban streets; if a cop had tried to pull us over, she wouldn't have stopped. Once we were home, Mom herded us down the basement stairs and into the fallout shelter, locking the door behind us. "Make yourselves comfortable. It's going to be awhile before we can come out," she said, snapping the deadbolt home.

With extensive work, we had transformed the old coal room. There were three metal frame bunkbeds, their heads against one wall, with just enough space to stand in between them. Gray steel shelves with glass jars of canned vegetables and gigantic plastic water cans lined the opposite wall, and a kitty litter-filled lavatory behind a vinyl shower curtain stood in a corner. The shelter was small and damp, and a heavy, musty smell lingered no matter what we did to air it out. It was dark, dismal and uncomfortable, and I dreaded going down there when it was my turn to check the flashlight batteries or empty and refill the water cans.

"I know we have everything we need," Mom said.

"How long?" I asked, rubbing my arms; I wore a short sleeved t-shirt, and my arms were covered in goose pimples.

"A couple of weeks," Mom said, cheerful and smiling. "Maybe a month."

"I can't stay down here for a month. It smells bad."

"Would you rather be out in the radioactive fallout?" Ron asked.

"You're such a baby," Ken said.

"I'm so sick of listening to you whine," Sandy said. "That's all you ever do."

"Anna, you know we have to do this," Grace said.

"It's stay down here or die, Anna," Mom said, calmly, stating a fact.

My parents went out of their way to make nuclear war seem a normal, acceptable, every day risk, like car accidents, muggings or food poisoning. They didn't scare us into preparedness; we were never woken in the dark and told to run for the shelter because the Soviets were on their way, or threatened with immediate incineration if we didn't hurry. Our parents never tried to correct our bad behavior by threatening to lock us out of the shelter when the invasion happened. My mother didn't repeat her father's Hiroshima horror stories for us when we were children, although we got them first-hand after we moved to St. Louis.

"Certainly, people will suffer and die," Mom and Dad told us, "but only because they have chosen not to take precautions, or don't believe the threat is real. Only people who don't know what to do or are foolish enough to live in target areas will suffer."

As long as we lived in the middle of nowhere, isolated from facts, isolated from people, it was easy to believe what Mom and Dad told us: that surviving a nuclear attack was purely a matter of personal choice, personal responsibility. Once my father died and we moved to St. Louis, once we were exposed to TV news and public schools, nuclear attack seemed more likely, but survival became less certain. We were now in an immediate target area, susceptible to the heat and blast of a nuclear bomb, which we knew was the most difficult to survive, but we remained hopeful. Then, on that March afternoon, I finally understood what was at stake, and just what survival might mean.

We waited. Ron, Sandy and Ken stretched out on their bunks and read by flashlight, and Grace curled up on the floor and slept. Mom sat cross-legged at the foot of a bunk, a portable radio in her lap. I paced back and forth, stepping over Grace, kicking at the stained, gray, cement walls. I felt trapped, doomed, like I would never get out of that dark, musty room; each time I crossed the room it felt smaller, darker, mustier, until it seemed the walls would collapse in on me.

"Sit down, Anna," Mom said, looking up from the radio. "Stay calm.
Take shallow breaths through your nose. You'll use less oxygen that way." They were all so calm, breathing through their noses, reading magazines and books as if this was normal, as if they were waiting for dinner on just another afternoon.

I gulped air, trying to calm myself. Soon I was hysterical and sobbing, using more than my fair share of oxygen. I was absolutely certain that we'd walk out of the shelter in three weeks and find a devastated and poisoned world. The thought that any minute now, people would evaporate, just boil away, or, best case, would soon be dying from radiation poisoning, was terrible. All I know is ending, I thought, picturing people from school. I thought of my grandparents and their neighbors, and I could see everyone, everything, vanishing in a blinding flash of light. Being safe in our shelter seemed selfish, and I wondered how my family could consign everyone else to radioactive fallout so calmly. And I was ashamed of not being calm and accepting like Ron, Sandy, Ken and Grace. When I tried explaining my fears and dread to my family, they told me to grow up, to stop being a sentimental baby, to quit whining, to be a survivor.

Mom ignored my tears. She fiddled with the tuning knob on the radio, waiting for the static on all bands that would signal a massive missile bombardment. She smiled and joked the whole time. "What do you call a man with no arms and no legs who hangs on the wall?" she asked. "Art. What do you call a man with no arms and no legs in a swimming pool? Bob. Anna, the month isn't going to go any faster if you pace the entire time. How about the man with no arms and no legs who fell into boiling water? Stew."

We stayed in the dark musty cellar for five and a half hours; outside, the first beautiful spring day faded into night. I huddled in a corner, shaking with fear. My last day alive, or at least, my last normal day alive, I kept thinking, and I wasted it at school.

Still fiddling with the radio knobs, my mother came across a talk show, where reporters and callers were denouncing the President's on-air joke as tasteless. One of the callers said, "It would have served us right if the Soviets had retaliated." "You're absolutely right. It was fool-hardy, stupid, and nothing less than unpresidential," a journalist said.

"Mom?" Grace asked, standing, sounding bored. "Can I go out and play?"

Mom stayed where she was, the radio on her lap. "I just don't understand it." Her voice was low, and she shook her head.

I struggled with the deadbolt; when the door swung open I ran upstairs and through the house, turning on lights, radios, the TV, proving the world still existed. My family followed me but they moved slowly, as if they were disappointed. They wanted the challenge of trying to survive a nuclear war, wanted to prove they could.

In the months after the false alarm, Mom grew nervous about my ability to survive, and she brought every little failing, my lost keys and forgotten chores, back to my panic in the shelter. "How are you going to be prepared for the things that really matter if you can't handle the small things?"

"I don't know." I shrugged, tried to ignore her, kept my eyes glued to the TV screen, though I wasn't really paying attention to it.

"This is serious, Anna."

I got off the couch and left the room. Mom followed me out of the living room, so I went upstairs. "Anna, I'm talking to you. What do you do for a broken femur? How do you navigate your way out of the woods if you're lost without a compass or a map? How do you change a spare tire?" She stayed just a few steps behind me.

"I don't want to talk about it," I screamed, slamming my bedroom door in her face. My room was an awful, empty box, just a twin bed with a scratchy Army surplus wool blanket across it, a battered dresser, a fire extinguisher in one corner, and a flashlight in case of power loss next to the bed. I hated it, but wasn't motivated enough to change anything. I locked the door, and just in case Mom knew how to pick the lock, shoved the dresser in front of it. It was an old, heavy dresser, solid walnut, the finish scratched and gouged; sliding it across the floor took all my strength.

Just thinking that she might know how to pick a lock was chilling. I'll never be able to hide from her, I thought, straining to move the dresser.

Mom stood on the other side of the door, twisting and rattling the knob. "Anna Louisa Greer, you come out here right now and answer my question. What do you do for a broken femur?" She was quiet for a minute. I pictured her standing with her hands on her hips, glaring at the door. "What would you do if there was a tornado, right now?" she called. "Do you know what it would sound like?"

My grandparents had given me a boom box, and I turned it on now, for the first time, twisted the volume all the way up. There was a horrible noise as two staticky stations came in, voices and music fading in and out, buzzing and hissing, and I put my hands over my ears. Mom pounded on the door, hard, with both fists. "If you don't start taking these things seriously, you won't be a survivor."

My brothers and sisters crowded into the hall with her. I didn't hear their voices so much as sense their presence, because if Mom was yelling at me, they were sure to come running. I stood in the middle of my bare room and flipped them off with both hands. I would have been scared to do it to their faces, but with the door between us, I felt brave. "Just leave me the fuck alone," I screamed.

The next morning, after I came downstairs, sullen and hungry, my stomach growling, Mom and Ron removed my bedroom door from its hinges.

I moped that spring, and all summer long. My brothers and sisters kept telling me to snap out of it. "You're pathetic, Anna," Ron said. "Think of the big picture. Think of what we need to do after the nuclear war."

Sandy pulled me aside. "Look, the important thing is to be a survivor while everyone else is incinerated." There was malice in her voice, and it was obvious that she believed her entire graduating class deserved to be obliterated.

"God, Anna, do something besides moping around, would you?" Ken said. "Why don't you help me clean out the shelter and refill the water cans?"

"Get over it," was Grace's advice. "So what if that wasn't the attack? There'll be one soon. Think of it as a dry run."

I knew they were right, but late into the summer the knowledge that I'd failed was always pressing down on me like the damp July heat. That was disturbing enough, but the questions forming in the back of my mind were worse. Was it possible to be prepared for everything, every little quirk of circumstance, every major catastrophe, every minor mishap? Would it be worth it to remain alive, while everyone else died? Could I bear to spend months, maybe years, in a fallout shelter, and what would the world be like when we emerged from our dank, dirty shelter?

I tried to block it all out. I anesthetized myself with TV, watching whatever was on, soap operas, sports, game shows, anything so I didn't have to think. Then one Saturday afternoon Mom found me curled up on the couch, watching *Dr. Strangelove* on cable.

"I don't see why you're so selfish," Mom said, twisting the TV knob to off. "Get out and do something; go weed the garden. You'll feel better if you do something useful."

"I don't see why we bother with a garden," I said. It was 95 degrees, with the kind of humidity that presaged sudden violent storms. "There are grocery stores. There are produce stands."

Mom took a step back, stunned by my sudden questioning of the basic tenets of survival. "What—Anna, you know why we grow and can our own food. After a nuclear attack, there won't be any grocery stores. You'll need to know how to provide for yourself." Mom pushed me out the back door. She put the hoe in my hand. "Don't come back until every single weed is gone," she said, going inside, and locking the door for good measure.

I pulled weeds with my bare hands; it felt good to hurt something, to destroy something living, even if it was just spurge and dandelions. Heat rose from the damp dirt, and the sun beat down on my back. My skin stung from sweat and sunburn, and I resented every square inch of the garden, hated the time and effort it took.

"No one else at school has a garden," I said. "No one else cans their own food." I wasn't looking forward to the long days of canning, the steaming water bath pushing the humidity past tolerable, the heat in the kitchen past 100 degrees. I thought about the meticulous slicing of carrots and cucumbers, cutting kernels from corncobs, squeezing tomatoes out of their skins, and packing all of it into hot, sterile jars. Mom favored an assembly line method, with all six of us crammed into the kitchen, and there was no escape.

"It's pointless, canning all that food." I was thinking about our afternoon in the fallout shelter. "We'd never survive. How can Mom be so stupid?" Once I said it I knew what had been bothering me since the afternoon in the shelter, and maybe since we'd moved to St. Louis.

We weren't going to survive.

Even in the middle of nowhere, we wouldn't have survived.

"Lies, lies! It's all lies!" I tugged on a tomato vine, fighting to pull it from the dirt. It gave way and sent me sprawling into a tangle of plants— beans, corn, peppers—and showered dirt clods around me. Everything stood out. The lies my parents had told us. The false hopes they'd nurtured. And the stark truth: we were doomed, just like everyone else. Surviving a nuclear blast wasn't just a matter of personal responsibility and being prepared.

In a frenzy of rage and fear I destroyed the garden. I chopped up corn stalks with the hoe, tore runner beans from their strings, smashed tomatoes. My hoe took bites out of tall plants, left them maimed, oozing fluid and listing to one side. I pulled up half-grown onions and threw them against the side of the garage, and hacked into the hills where the potatoes were forming. I slaughtered the beets and their sticky, red juice spattered across my shins. In twenty minutes there was nothing but a trampled mess, the leaves slick under my feet, and a wet, vegetable smell in the air. I had destroyed an entire season's worth of produce.

I was panting and surveying the damage when the screen door banged shut and Mom came out to make sure I was working. She took in the destruction of the neat rows and ripening vegetables. She screamed but couldn't form words, gasped for air and screamed again, a long howl like she'd been maimed. The others came running.

"What happened?" Sandy asked, looking at the smashed vegetables, the trampled plants, and me, hoe in hand.

"She did it," Mom said, trying to catch her breath. "Why, Anna? Why?"

"Are you insane?" Ken looked panicked, like he might cry. "How could you?"

"We'll starve." Sandy knelt and brought up a handful of smashed beets, carrots and cabbage, then looked at me. "There'll be a nuclear war and we'll starve."

Ron's fists were clinched, and his voice was a low hiss. "It'll be your fault when we die. You traitor. You've killed us."

Grace just sobbed and slid about in the wreckage, looking for something salvageable.

"Oh please," I said, scornful. Ten or fifteen minutes later, I might have begun to feel guilty, to doubt my actions, but when Mom and the others confronted me, I was still angry, and newly empowered. I wiped my face on my sleeve and looked at them; they were showing more emotion over the garden than they had when Dad died. "We can't survive a nuclear war. Radiation takes hundreds of years to decay."

They seemed to vibrate from shock and disbelief. Everyone's eyes were wide open, stricken. Grace's lower lip quivered.

"Have you lost your mind? How can you say that?" Mom asked, hands on her hips, mouth hanging open.

I shrugged. "It's true. We'd never make it."

Debra Frogly   Healthy

You –
you mass-media, advertising-junkie, money-making
rat-race culture, with your skinny white women and your
products to make beautiful more beautiful, and the rest-
of-us well, maybe, pretty. Your cosmetic surgery
creates a plastic reality. Your fashions change each
season, mid-season; if I have that look, that image, I will
be beautiful—how dare you, you image-addicted fallacy.

You –
you demand, you desire, you pimp; more more
more we prostitute style, our beauty sold. You will kill
us with the gloss of your magazines, acid that corrodes
what is truly beautiful about all of us. I want
to throw my blood at you, to make you see, make you
think; make you taste me and know what you have
created. I will be cleansed. You will be taught.

You –
you dare to presume to possess me with your
conformity. I possess me, my choices, my life, my beauty.
Take it all, take it in and know we are all beautiful,
know beauty has many faces. Yet you need to reduce
it to one—why? Beauty is genuine, innate. Who do you
think you are—God? Is this healthy, are you healthy?
Tell me you are and I will tell you, you are beautiful.

You –
you disgust me. I will not make it easy for you.
I will breathe, shout, love, dance naked around
the fire under a bright full moon; my freckled skin
will glisten with sweat, and you will watch and want me,
you fucked-up 21st Century Western World. I wanted
what you want once—but now I am beautiful.
Healthy

t

Sophia Longhi   The Lesson

Emma Binkum sux cock
Becca 4 Jamie
Becca 4 Adam

Rachel Warson, hunched over with stomach cramps, sat on the cold plastic toilet seat, having nothing better to do than to read the graffiti on the door. The scabby red paint was flaking off and one particular bit was annoying her. She leaned forward and picked it off.

Becca is a slag
I luv Warren
For sex call 074947001258

001258...

"What the fuck! Slags," she mumbled as she searched for a pen in her schoolbag.

Rachel scratched over her mobile number, taking away more of the red paint and revealing the old crayon-blue paint underneath. She envisioned Bryony and Marie's faces. She knew it must have been them—they had written it on the desk in science and everyone had laughed.

When she had finished scratching out her number, all that remained was the raw wood. She carved into the door.

Bryony Matthews takes it up the arse + so does Marie Snyder

It took her about ten minutes to complete her masterpiece and, with a sense of accomplishment, she sat back on the toilet seat and grinned. Suddenly, she drew in a sharp breath. Feeling the pain in her stomach again, her grin had quickly been replaced by a grimace. Worry waved over her like the nausea, but then she ignored it, like she always did.

What could she do now to amuse herself? She looked at her watch. 11.12am. The bell rings at five to. She had forty-three minutes to kill. The second hand jerked tediously.

Rachel never usually skived Maths. She fancied the teacher too much. Mr Wallis—with his cheeky smile and sexy baby-blues; she couldn't believe she was missing out on him today. It wasn't the fact that she hadn't done her homework—Lucy would have let her copy hers anyway. Instead, it was this bloody... well, what really was it? She hated the term;

the term itself made her feel sick. 'Morning sickness'. Worry sickness more like.

She counted along with the second hand in her head. Seven. Eight. Nine. Ten.

There was a creak. Rachel heard the door swing open and she held her breath. There was a ritual she performed every time she skived, just so that no-one got suspicious. She lifted up the toilet seat as though she had just got into the toilets herself. She stayed on the toilet, biding her time, fumbling noisily with the loo roll. The other person flushed. She heard them wash their hands and when the drier went, Rachel flushed. The door opened and quickly slammed shut.

She took a deep breath that was suddenly forced out by the stabbing pain in her stomach. She clutched her tummy and rubbed it. Then, she had the immediate urge to puke.

Rachel suspected she might have been pregnant for some time now. Maybe a couple of months. No... she went to Blackpool in the February and now it was the beginning of June... She didn't really know because she always stopped herself from thinking about it. She probably wasn't even pregnant at all. Tests were too expensive and absent periods were easy to forget about – there's just nothing there. It was quite common for girls to have irregular periods at her age anyway.

After five wretches, Rachel reached for the flush. She sat back on the toilet and looked down at her bulging stomach. She poked at it. Guilty tears threatened to wet her eyes but she blinked them back. Rachel was aware that it couldn't be fat—she had hardly been eating anything recently, hoping that whatever was in there, if it was, would shrivel up and starve to death. But the baggy jumpers were still being pulled on.

Tick... tick...

11.28am. Just twenty-seven minutes to go. Rachel wondered what they were doing today. Algebra? Who cares? She bet Lucy was sitting at the front with a great view of Mr Wallis. Cow.

Lucy was her best friend; still, she even kept this secret from her. It was all her fault too. Lucy had asked her parents if it would be alright for Rachel to join them in Blackpool. Always going on about boys; sex this, sex that. Just because Lucy's on three and she's only on one.

The piercing pain again. This time it grabbed her from inside. Rachel thrust forward with the pain, hitting her head on the toilet door. There was something wrong, she could feel it. She began to cry. What if she was going to die? She had to get out—to tell someone.

Rachel grappled for the lock, but her hand was shaking. Her grip tightened around it with the next pulse of agony. Wait. There was something wet between her legs.

Panicking and scared, Rachel lifted up her skirt. Red. She brushed her trembling hand against it and looked at her fingertips. Blood.

Rachel pulled up the toilet seat and sat down, her head hanging between her knees with the pain. It... the baby. The baby? What if it's coming? Oh God.

She felt the automatic urge to push down, to get the pain out. She was barely there with herself as she looked down into the toilet. Nothing made sense. Dark red water, almost black. Broken lumps of black-red. Whatever it was looked like the giblets out of a chicken that her mum boiled up. Where was the baby?

Rachel silenced her tears. Where was the baby? Rachel threw up on the floor.

The sound of the second hand jabbed in her ear.

The blood was still dripping into the toilet. Her stomached ached and probed at her but she felt numb. Empty. Soulless. She stared at the red paint on the door.

The bell rang. There was a bustle of voices and a slamming of doors.

Corporal Pullman approached his squad vehicle, cursing under his breath. Lance Corporal Brooklyn lay on his stomach in the shade under the camo netting reading a tattered Danielle Steele. He didn't look up when the squad leader dropped his Kevlar helmet in the sand next to his head.

Pullman stopped short and looked at Private First Class Rhodes with angered amazement. The junior Marine was kneeling in the sand before a cook stove and proudly wore a smile under a soot-covered face.

"Now you don't have to tinker around with this old piece of shit anymore, Corporal," he beamed, "I fixed it right up."

Pullman dragged his feet through the sand over to Rhodes, put his hands on his hips and leaned over.

"Wellll, is *that* so?" the squad leader asked the top of Rhodes's short, sand-dusted hair. "I guess I oughta be grateful or something, huh? Bein' that you saved me so much time and effort and all, right? Maybe I should ask Gunny to give you a field promotion or give you a night off from firewatch. Would you like that? Is that what you want, PFC?"

Rhodes looked to Brooklyn but the other Marine had vanished, leaving his pulp romance to flutter on its back in the desert breeze. Rhodes raised his face to Pullman's. The Corporal was sunburned with rage. Permanent five o'clock shadow covered the older man's face ear-to-ear and a thick tuft of black chest hair poked out from the top of his stretched out t-shirt. Rhodes knew the squad leader's eyes were burning a hole through his brain even though they were hidden behind dark prescription sunglasses.

"Let's just see how well you fixed my stove, PFC."

Pullman took off his desert camo top and threw it against the Humvee. It landed in the sand and stood on its own, the salt from sweat keeping it stiff. Pullman dropped to his knees and picked the stove up in his hands, turning it in all directions to see what changes had been made. He placed it on the ground, pumped it a few times, opened the fuel line and lit the burner with an MRE match. It instantly came to life: a strong, even flame that actually strengthened and weakened with an adjustment by the knob on the side. Most amazing of all, the burner emitted almost no black smoke even though the fuel they were forced to use was JP8, jet fuel.

PFC Rhodes beamed with the success of his efforts.

"See, Corporal? I got it working like a charm. Now you don't have to waste all day trying to fix it." He smiled shyly at the squad leader. Pullman's face was slack and emotionless.

The Corporal turned the burner off and the stove let out a small pop as the remaining fuel in the lines was consumed, then the flame disappeared and everything was quiet.

"Great fucking job," Pullman whispered and he threw the stove against the side of the Humvee. It hit the vehicle like a sack of canned vegetables. Rhodes fell back in the sand on his elbows in surprise.

Pullman stood, rushed to the stove, and gave it a kick for good measure.

"You think I don't know how to fix a fucking *stove*, boot?"

Rhodes recoiled at each word and pushed himself away from his squad leader with his desert boots.

"I have dismantled and assembled that stove every day for the last three months just to keep myself fucking *sane*! I don't need your fucking help, worm, I know what the fuck I'm doing. And I know what *you're* gonna be doing now too." An evil smile, often seen, came to Pullman's face. "You'll be on firewatch every night until we leave Saudi Arabia for the sweet U. S. of A. Hell, you did such a good job with my stove, I know we'll all sleep a little easier knowing you're on the job. The whole platoon will breathe a sigh of relief knowing you got their backs while they dream of being ass-deep in pussy."

Pullman picked up the stove, beat it against the vehicle to get the sand out and dropped it on his starchy desert shirt.

"Now, go dig me a foxhole, and it better be deep and wide like a fucking grave. I have a stove to fix."

One spring, in the seaside village of Genoa, it rained for so many days that people forgot the sun. They couldn't tell where the sea ended and where the world began because everything was wet; all food tasted like salt, and villagers often awoke with a seahorse beneath their pillow or a starfish clinging to their bare foot. Many fishermen were lost. Wives placed a candle in their windows. But they knew their dead husbands would wash ashore, floating face down with blue skin.

After the storm ended, the sun broke through the clouds, warmed the sea, and baked the zinc rooftops. One man was left with the sound of rain in his ears long after it stopped. The sea swallowed fourteen ships. Thirty-two men were missing. And the only animals to survive were the parakeets locked inside cages. Wreckage covered the sand, the stink of dead fish was everywhere, and at dusk a great crowd gathered at the shoreline, for it seemed many centuries had passed since they had watched the sunset.

That afternoon, the boy Maris asked his father for permission to search the beach for treasures. "You may go," the father said, smoking his bamboo pipe, nostrils steaming. He was a widowed man, who earned a humble living from his small junk shop in town. "But remember!" he said. "You're no thief! Should you find anything that belongs to the sea, be sure to throw it back from where it came."

"I promise, Papa."

Traveling south along the beach left Maris feeling drowned, for in every direction there were signs of shipwrecks. He saw canvas sails tattered and soaked, wooden rudders encrusted in barnacles, and splintered ship wheels with rosaries tied to the handlebars.

When the moon rose, the shoreline was covered in a bluish air that made the sand glitter like crushed glass. He came to a part of the beach covered in jellyfish. Summers spent swimming near the reef taught him to keep his distance from these beauties, their deadly lights blinking on and off like heartbeats. He stepped carefully in his cork sandals. By morning they would be deflated sacks cooked by the sun.

Up ahead he saw a dark shape lying on the sand among the jellies. At first he thought it was a figurehead torn lose from a ship's prow. Then it moved, and he suspected it was a castaway. But when he drew closer he saw it was neither. It was a woman lying face down in a shallow pool and where her legs should have been was the tail of a fish.

Maris's stomach became filled with ice. At the sound of his approach

175

she raised herself on her right arm and lifted her head with a tremendous effort. Her long black hair fell past her shoulders, dipping into the pool she was marooned in. She had no eyebrows and no eyelashes, giving her face an expression of perpetual surprise. Her left arm was broken, bruised the color of eggplant, lying limp and heavy in its socket. Below her ears were three slits like knife wounds. These were her gills which opened and closed like wet lips. Her eyes were her only earthly feature, for they were the eyes of a horse, black and eternal.

Using one of her webbed fingers, she began writing in the sand a series of frantic, unrecognizable hieroglyphics. But each symbol dissolved in seawater and she gave up. Suddenly she pointed towards the distant shoreline and opened her mouth to speak. But all that came was a wheezing hiss of air and her flapping blue tongue.

Maris's heart beat wildly. Her muscular tail, infested with barnacles and tangled in a net of seaweed, was cut in so many places that the blood pooled between her scales, and because she had spent a lifetime swimming through nautical gardens, her wounds smelled like flowers.

Aside from an albatross circling above, Maris was alone. He wished his father were here.

Last winter a great humpback whale washed ashore. He was so enormous he divided the beach in two halves. No one knew what to do with him and for many days the women of the village, wearing scarves and coats, poured buckets of water over his body to keep him from dying.

Maris's father took his son to visit the humpback one afternoon. The creature's shadow covered the entire beach. Maris pressed his ear to the whale's belly and listened to the humming and bubbling. The beast's mighty lungs sounded like a hurricane bottled up inside a jar. Then he approached the whale's head and the monstrous black eye rolled in its socket and fixed on him. A women, her knuckles raw and cracked, her eyes pink from the salty air, passed him a bucket of sea water. "Keeps her from drying up," she said. Then he realized the creature was female. All the more sad, Maris thought. It was not her fault for being so big and heavy.

"You don't belong here," he whispered to the whale. Maris splashed some sea water across the whale's skin, and before leaving, he petted the beast just below her eye.

The next morning those few remaining women who fought against the cold—exhausted and aching, hands frozen, lips dried out—were outnumbered by the drunken fishermen who marched across the beach with clubs. By noon, the whale was dead. Not long after, the whalers arrived with their tools and knives to strip the flesh and collect the blubber. Maris, watching from his window, saw the bloody-pink skin shining wetly in the sunlight.

"A mighty shame," his father said. "No lure was cast to catch that whale. She was an accident."

Now he understood that it was up to him to save the woman with the fish tail. The albatross circled twice more and glided off towards the moon.

Kneeling beside her, he rolled her onto her back. Her skin was coated in slime. He had never seen the unclothed body of a woman before and the sight caused his heart to beat quickly. Her stomach was smooth and below that place where her bellybutton should have been, her turquoise scales began as natural as anything.

She did not scream or bite at him, but instead her features composed themselves like a painting. She looked upon him with such gratitude he thought she might weep. He had to be careful of her broken arm. With both hands he pulled her up by her good wrist, heaved her entire torso onto his hunched-over back, and let her tail fin drag in the sand behind them, so that in the end he carried her like a great sack of gifts slung over his shoulder. They were cheek to cheek, and as he began to lug her, her fluttering gills brushed the nape of his neck like the wing of a bird and he knew she was alive. If she dies, he thought, I will stay with her until her gills stop moving.

His ears pounded with blood. The shoreline, which had seemed so near only a moment ago, appeared an unreachable distance. The sand was so wet he sank down to his ankles, his cork sandals were pulled off, leaving him barefoot. He wished for the candlelit comforts of his father's shanty, his mattress stuffed with goose feathers near the open window where the sea breezes lifted the lace curtains. Suddenly, he stepped onto one of the jellyfish.

His foot was pricked by a thousand needles and together, he and the woman pitched sideways. They slammed into the sand. Bright pinwheels of light flashed before his eyes. The bones in his leg felt electrified and a scattering of blisters covered his foot, bubbling up like white warts. The woman lay just outside arm's reach. She will surely die, he thought. His eyes watered, the moon blurred, and he prayed for the distant satellite to work its magic and bring in the tide. Just enough to wet her skin, he thought, and help her home.

Dragging her broken arm the woman crawled like a seal towards his foot. Then she opened her mouth. Her long blue tongue uncoiled and began licking the boy's foot. He could hardly breathe. Her tongue snaked between his toes, coated his skin in a gelatin, and leeched the poison until the pain vanished. Then his bones felt complete and he stood once more.

He was too tired to heave her across his back, so he dragged her by the wrist, leaving a shallow dugout in the sand. She began to sing in a strange language, a song with the funereal tones of winter. I wish you were mine, he thought. Together they'd travel to a faraway island, live peacefully in the sun, and bathe nude along warm beaches.

When they reached the shoreline Maris let go of the woman's wrist and fell to his knees to catch his breath. The warm waves splashed all around him. The woman had stopped singing. Lying on her side, she looked asleep. He touched her shoulder. It was cold, and he knew she was dead. Her gills did not flutter. Her gray eyes reflected the moon perfectly. And her blue lips remained posed in song.

He picked up her wrist and dragged her further into the foaming surf. She slid smoothly into the water. As if death had hollowed her bones, she floated upon the surface like a sleeping queen. He kept one hand on her stomach and waded out until the salty water met his lips. He hesitated to take his hand off her stomach. But it did not matter. The waves had an impatient motion that carried her quickly away. In that silent moment he watched her drift off, suspended between sea and stars, until she was a dot on the horizon and vanished below the green shadows of the sea.

N

We weave between tables, singing "yo amo bilar"
Leo puts his hands on my hips as I swing them
And everyone sips from cold bottles of Corona

Latin rhythms push us harder and faster
I twirl beneath ceiling fans amongst Cuban men
As we weave between tables, singing "yo amo bilar"

Old ladies sit eating bowls of Sopa Negra
I receive cheers from the guys, but not the women
And everyone sips from cold bottles of Corona

Movement blurs the painted face of Che Guevara
Hues of blue, white and red begin to merge and blend
As we weave between tables, singing "you amo bilar"

Sam slaps his bongos, Jorge strums his guitar
Hips and thighs twist and wind; a teasing salsa rhythm
And everyone swigs from cold bottles of Corona

Our feet stamp and dance the path of cha-cha-cha
Leo grips my waist in a passionate clinch, and then
We weave between tables, singing "yo amo bilar"
And everyone guzzles back cold bottles of Corona

Biographies

Katie Corboy is a Chicago girl through and through. She received her MFA in Creative Writing from Columbia College Chicago in May 2007, where she was Assistant Artistic Director of the Story Week Festival of Writers, coordinator on Creative Non-fiction Week, tutor in Fiction Writing Skills, managing editor of *Fictionary*, and editor on the student anthology *Hair Trigger 27*. Her writing has appeared in *Fictionary, The Story Week Reader, Hair Trigger 27,* and on writingcompetition.com, for which she won first place. In 2003, she received the Academic Excellence Award, a Columbia scholarship. She taught creative writing to fifth graders at Paul Revere Intermediate School for two semesters. Corboy also participated in the Summer Abroad program in Prague and the Adaptation program on the CBS lot in Los Angeles. Currently, she is the volunteer Event Coordinator for The Keep On Keeping On Foundation, Grant Writing Intern at Literacy Chicago, and a literary media aide with Midwest Media. She is represented by the Caren Johnson Literary Agency regarding a novel-in-progress. One of her fondest memories of the exchange program was witnessing the kick-ass ingenuity of the students at Bath Spa University at work during Ambidextrous Night in the Student Union.

Felicity Crentsil graduated from Bath Spa University with a BA Honours in Creative Writing and will not leave. She is currently studying her Masters in Writing for Young People. She acted as an E-Mentor during the 2007 Man Booker Prize for Young Writer's trial and is interested in working with young people to encourage reading and writing. She is currently working on her first novel and enjoying part-time employment as a Library Assistant.

Debra Frogley has a BA Honours in English Literature with Creative Writing from Bath Spa University. During her final year, she worked on this anthology project and served as an e-mail E-Mentor for the Man Booker Prize Young Writer's Competition, helping her mentee to critique, redraft and edit her work. Now working for a solicitors by day, by night she is writing her first children's novel. Before returning to university, Debra worked as a retail manager for several years but never gave up her love of writing. She attended a vocational evening course in creative writing, and has had two poems published in small press anthologies. Debra has written a number of short stories and poems, and is currently working on her application for a Master of Arts in Writing for Young People at Bath Spa University.

Liz Henley is a graduate of Bath Spa University and lives in Aylesbury. During her final year she was Press Relations and Marketing Officer for Ambidextrous, the university's creative society, where she designed all advertising, interviewed local bands and wrote articles for the student newspaper. She was also the creator of the paper's comic strip, Student Stick Theatre and wrote a column about fun things to find online. During last summer, she was hired as a reviewer for *ThreeWeeks* magazine at the Edinburgh Fringe Festival and plans on returning again this year. She is currently writing a children's fantasy novel and working towards her dream job in publishing.

Geoff Hyatt is a graduate of Western Michigan University's Creative Writing Workshop and an MFA Fiction Writing candidate of Columbia College Chicago. He currently works as a writer and creative consultant for Star Farm Productions. His fiction has appeared in *Hair Trigger, The Harrow, Thuglit,* and elsewhere. Geoff has fond memories of his time in Bath, discussing of the melancholia of pheasants and the mysteries of brown sauce. He still hasn't been to Legoland.

Lyndsey Melling was born and raised in deepest Devon, finally escaping to study at Bath Spa University in 2004. She graduated with a First in Creative Writing and Sociology, and continues to work in Bath. She enjoys life drawing, filmmaking, and generally making a nuisance of herself. She hopes to have a continuing (and preferably paid) involvement with the University for many years to come.

M. R. Morrison is an Army Aviator stationed at Fort Rucker, AL. She graduated from Columbia College Chicago with a BFA in Fiction Writing and is currently at work on a novel in stories. She's been published in *Fine Lines Magazine, The Big Ugly Review* and *Hair Trigger.* She currently dyes her hair and no longer believes in mermaids.

Jessica M. Young is delighted to have worked with such fine artists and writers on this anthology. Jessica graduated with a Bachelor's Degree in Performance Studies from Northwestern University in 2002. She is pursuing a Masters of Fine Arts in Fiction Writing at Columbia College Chicago. She has published various short stories and reviews, and is an award recipient of the 2006 Fiction Contest held by the Union League Civic & Arts Foundation of Chicago. Jessica has served as a teaching artist for high school students in numerous classes and workshops, and she teaches reading to children and adults across the country. She is currently an adjunct faculty member at Columbia College Chicago and lives in Chicago.

Anna Freeman is in her second year of a Creative Writing degree at Bath Spa. She lives in Bristol in a flat so small that it is invisible to the naked eye, and hopes to be an astronaut when she grows up.

Chai-Pei "CP" Chang calls himself a Chicago boy, even during the time that he's lived in other cities and countries, and he'll continue to call himself that even after he moves again. He received his MFA in Creative Writing from Columbia College Chicago in the spring of 2007.

Sarah Parry graduated from Bath Spa University in 2007 and is training to be a primary school teacher. She doesn't normally tell sensible stories.

Dominic West is a graduate of Bath Spa University, where, in 2007, he gained a BA Honours degree in Creative Studies in English. He now lives in Cornwall, England, and is in the process of writing a collection of short stories entitled *Way Out*.

Teddie Goldenberg was born in Bangkok, raised in Washington DC, and lives in Chicago. He recently graduated from Columbia College Chicago with a BFA in Fiction Writing.

Emerson Leese, 33, is currently studying towards a MA in Creative Writing at Bath Spa University. He is near to completing his first collection of poetry, *The Serenity Prayer*.

Faren MacDonald hails from Vermont but often calls Chicago, where she goes to school, home. An undergraduate at Columbia College Chicago, she has only a few more credit hours to complete before she graduates from the Fiction Writing program.

Lyndall Henning, although currently living in Britain, grew up in South Africa where her story is set. She is currently halfway through her full time Masters in Creative Writing at Bath Spa University.

Gordon Egginton has just graduated from his BA and is currently studying for his MA in Creative Writing. He is working on his first novel as well as appearing regularly as a performance poet.

Daniel Prazer hails from North Canton, Ohio and lives in Chicago with his wife Ann. He is working on his thesis toward an MFA in Creative Writing at Columbia College Chicago.

Tracy Wall, who lives in Glastonbury, England, is married with twin daughters and works part-time as a freelance journalist while studying poetry for a Masters degree at Bath Spa University. She wrote the play *Life Class* while in her second year of her BA degree in English Literature and Creative Writing.

Jamison Spencer is from Richmond, VA (directly in front of the third grave of General Ap Hill), but lives in Chicago. He is an MFA student in Creative Writing at Columbia College Chicago.

Abby Keverne graduated from Bath Spa University in 2007. She is fascinated by different cultures and how art and writing can have strong links between one another worldwide. She hopes to explore this unity further in her future career.

Melanie Datz had a reasonably normal, fallout shelter-free, childhood in suburban Chicago. She is currently an MFA student in Creative Writing at Columbia College Chicago.

Sophia Longhi has a degree in Creative Studies in English. She lives in Bath where she is currently training to teach English Literature. Her plan for the future is to fulfil her ambitions, which have always been dominated by two desires: to write and to travel.

Joseph Marceau resides in Chicago with his girlfriend, Anna, and their Jack Russell terrier, Milo. He is pursuing his BFA in Fiction Writing at Columbia College Chicago.

Ryan Sinon was born and raised in the suburbs of Chicago. He is currently pursuing an MFA degree in Creative Writing at Columbia College Chicago.

Tamsyn Fallows was born in 1985 in South Africa, but grew up in Somerset, England. She lives in Bristol and is in her final year of a History and Creative Writing degree at Bath Spa University.